Information Gold Mine

Innovative
Uses of
Evaluation

PAUL W. MATTESSICH
SHELLY HENDRICKS
Wilder Research, Amherst H. Wilder Foundation

ROSS VELURE ROHOLT
Public Achievement Northern Ireland

T0160428

FIELDSTONE
ALLIANCE

SAINT PAUL
MINNESOTA

Fieldstone Alliance is committed to strengthening the performance of the nonprofit sector. Through the synergy of its consulting, training, publishing, and research and demonstration projects, Fieldstone Alliance provides solutions to issues facing nonprofits, funders, and the communities they serve. Fieldstone Alliance was formerly Wilder Publishing and Wilder Consulting departments of the Amherst H. Wilder Foundation. If you would like more information about Fieldstone Alliance and our services, please contact

Fieldstone Alliance
60 Plato Boulevard East, Suite 150
Saint Paul, MN 55107
800-274-6024
www.FieldstoneAlliance.org

If you have questions about Wilder Research, please contact

Wilder Research
Suite 210
1295 Bandana Boulevard North
Saint Paul, MN 55108
651-647-4600
www.wilder.org/research

Edited by Vincent Hyman
Designed by Kirsten Nielsen

Manufactured in the USA
First printing, June 2007

Library of Congress Cataloging-in-Publication Data
Mattessich, Paul W.
  Information gold mine : innovative uses of evaluation / by Paul W. Mattessich, Shelly Hendricks, and Ross VeLure Roholt.
    p. cm.
  ISBN-13: 978-0-940069-51-0
  ISBN-10: 0-940069-51-2
1. Nonprofit organizations--Management. 2. Nonprofit organizations--Evaluation. 3. Project management. I. Hendricks, Shelly. II. Roholt, Ross VeLure, 1970- III. Title.
  HD62.6.M383 2007
  658.4'038--dc22
                              2007014162

About the Authors

PAUL W. MATTESSICH, PhD, is executive director of Wilder Research at Amherst H. Wilder Foundation, which dedicates itself to improving the lives of individuals, families, and communities through applied research. Wilder Research has a staff of approximately seventy-five people, including evaluation researchers, survey interviewers, data analysts, administrative support staff, and others. Paul has been involved in applied social research since 1973, working with local, national, and international organizations. He has authored or coauthored more than two hundred publications and reports, including the second edition of the popular book *Collaboration: What Makes It Work* and *The Manager's Guide to Program Evaluation: Planning, Contracting, and Managing for Useful Results*. He received his PhD in sociology from the University of Minnesota.

SHELLY HENDRICKS, M.P.P., worked as a research associate at Wilder Research for three years, supporting evaluators on various research projects. Some of the topics Shelly worked on include child care in Minnesota, American Indian diabetes self-management, and emergency shelter use in Saint Paul. She received her bachelor's degree from McPherson College and her master's degree in public policy from the Hubert H. Humphrey Institute at the University of Minnesota. Hendricks currently works as a community organizer for a neighborhood association in Minneapolis.

ROSS VELURE ROHOLT, PhD, is the action research officer for Public Achievement Northern Ireland, which dedicates itself to inviting and supporting young people to create innovative solutions to the legacy of violence and learning about democracy. In this role, Ross has conducted annual internal evaluations and managed several external evaluations on different programmatic initiatives supported by the organization. He received his PhD in education from the University of Minnesota.

Acknowledgments

BOOKS DON'T JUST HAPPEN. They require a lot of work not only by the authors, but by others who play many different, unseen roles in the creation of the final product. We have benefited greatly from the contributions of others. We thank the David and Lucile Packard Foundation, which provided financial support as part of its initiative to improve the effectiveness of nonprofit organizations.

This book relied, first and foremost, on the willingness of organizational leaders and managers to share their stories with us. We searched for creative innovators—people who could take information about what they do and how well they do it and leverage that information to improve services, but also in other significant ways to further the missions of their organizations. We thank Carol Arthur, Angie Datta, Sally Hopper, Kristi Lahti-Johnson, the late Nancy Latimer, Ellen Sachs Leicher, Shelley Lester, Mike McGrane, Valentin Miafo-Donfack, Lesa Radtke, Dr. Lawanda Ravoira, Tony Rothschild, Carol Seidenkranz, Tanya Tull, Kay Washington, and Debbie Wilde.

At Wilder Research, several colleagues carried out important tasks during the time we conducted interviews, organized the information we had collected, and produced the final manuscript. Marta Murray-Close spent many hours at the beginning of the project, assisting in identifying organizations to contact and gathering some of the case example information. Deirdre Hinz also provided research assistance. Sheila Romero coordinated the editing of the final version of each case example, communicating with our informants to ensure accuracy. Marilyn Conrad and Jackie Campeau provided administrative support. Dan Mueller and Cheryl Holm-Hansen provided early input on the design of the project. Ela Rausch checked and edited the case studies for accuracy.

Our publisher, Vince Hyman, at Fieldstone Alliance, has capably brought to press a good number of books from Wilder Research. With this latest book, he offered once again wise insight and useful critiques that greatly improved its quality.

Contents

Introduction

"Evaluation has given us another dimension. Lots of programs have touchy-feely stories. We have those too, and we do good work, just like other programs. But I can tell you what we do and what impacts it has in the scientific language of this business. This ability has given me more confidence in being bold about talking with people who have financial resources, in doing public relations, and in being assertive in asking for referrals. I feel like I really have solid ground to stand on. Not just me but my board as well. It's really given us confidence in our organization."

—Debbie Wilde, Executive Director, YouthZone

THESE WORDS COME FROM the executive director of a nonprofit organization. In Chapter 3, she enthusiastically describes the use of program evaluation research in her organization—for improving the quality of its services, as you might expect, but also for other purposes such as public relations, educating consumers, influencing policy, and motivating staff.

This book highlights the creativity and professional leadership of this person and others. It is written with the hope that the stories of these nonprofit organizations can inspire more organizations to use program evaluation, as well as other forms of applied research, to accomplish tasks that will increase their strength and their impacts. It's a book for the non-technicians—for the users, the actors, the decision makers, the managers, and the strategists.

If you have had any type of involvement with nonprofit, charitable organizations (and government agencies as well) during recent years, you have very likely had experiences like the following:

- You have heard many references to "outcomes" and "results."

- You have heard strategic planning consultants and motivational speakers state that organizations must "focus on results" and "reward success."

- You may have received an introduction to, or perhaps even extensive training in, "logic models." If so, you probably know about inputs, activities, outputs, and outcomes.

- If you have written a grant request for funding from a foundation or a government organization, you are probably familiar with the "evaluation component" of a proposal.

An "outcome" orientation has infused the nonprofit and government world. The vocabulary of outcomes has become more and more a part of the lexicon of nonprofit and government organizations.

- Increasingly, those who supply funding for programs require that program operators conduct formal program evaluation.

- Increasingly, the voting public has demanded that organizations receiving government money "prove their worth."

- Increasingly, programs in human services, education, arts, public safety, health, community development, and other fields have taken responsibility for measuring their activities and their impacts.

"Evidence-based practice"— selecting services to offer and tailoring services to specific patients or clients based on research evidence on effectiveness—has become a valuable standard in much of our healthcare system. Human service and education professionals have begun to adopt it as well.

Consumers have always had an interest in understanding whether services they may use can produce positive results. They, too, have begun to demand more information, more "accountability," from service providers. Advocacy organizations have pressured service delivery organizations to gather and publicly report service effectiveness information.

Amidst all of this, you have probably asked yourself: Has the increased interest in evaluating programs and measuring results, along with the increased effort this entails, actually improved the effectiveness of our organizations? Has it resulted in more benefits for clients, consumers, and the general public?

Organizations have done a lot of program evaluation during the past few decades. Have we used the things we have learned through all of that evaluation to full advantage? Have practitioners and organization managers taken advantage of evaluation findings for making improvements within their own organizations? Have they taken advantage of evaluation findings for influencing policy and legislation? Have they taken advantage of evaluation findings for marketing themselves to the community, strengthening their requests for funding, or other important tasks?

What about organizations making use of the knowledge produced by others? Have they taken advantage of the studies conducted by their colleagues in other organizations, or have they taken advantage of the articles and books that have compiled these findings from multiple organizations into principles for better management and practice?

Probably only to a small extent.

On the plus side, many organizations have made good use of evaluation findings. They have attempted to identify the best possible service practices by blending research evidence with the wisdom acquired through the experience of their staff. They have integrated the processes of evaluation research and service delivery so that they continually look for and test new ways, large and small, to serve their clients or improve the well-being of large numbers of people in their communities.

Many other organizations, though, have not woven program evaluation into their everyday work. In fact, the majority of organizations that deliver community-oriented services (health, education, or arts and culture, for example) do not systematically evaluate their own service outcomes. In addition, many of these organizations make no use of published studies of services in order to obtain new ideas or improve their effectiveness.

Moreover, service providers have probably only scratched the surface when it comes to using evaluation information as a tool for advancing organizations beyond improving their service effectiveness. For example, we often overlook opportunities to use evaluation research findings to educate the public and policymakers, to educate potential consumers of our services, to market an organization, to motivate staff, and to accomplish other significant tasks that could benefit organizations and the people they serve.

This book invites readers to make productive use of program evaluation information within nonprofit organizations. Through a small amount of explanation, plus a large number of examples, we hope to illustrate how organizations have not just done program evaluation, but have *used* program evaluation as a valuable, powerful tool.

The dark side of evaluation: Information waste dumps

Perhaps you are skeptical about the use of evaluation findings. Maybe you have seen program evaluation studies used only for accountability, not for ongoing program improvement. For example, a funder demanded a report, someone produced that report, and nobody ever had much use for it. Maybe you know about evaluation reports that languished on the shelf without any readers.

One of the authors of this book travels and lectures frequently, and he appeared on a panel at a conference of health professionals from throughout the United States. During the question and answer session, a member of the audience approached the microphone and criticized a panel member (fortunately, not this author!) for promoting evaluation in a way that was "abstract, tendentious, and irrelevant" to most people. The audience member framed the program evaluation experiences of his organization—a health advocacy organization—as an "unnecessary obstacle" to the accomplishment of its mission to improve the health and well-being of individuals within its state.

It's understandable if you are skeptical about the potential of program evaluation to produce benefits for you. You are not alone. Often, program evaluation research has not adequately involved stakeholders to ensure their ownership in the design. Consequently, program evaluation has not always provided the information that potential users could use, and it has missed the opportunity to serve as a resource for program improvement and other important activities.

Enlightened evaluation: Results-rich gold mines

Fortunately, many program evaluators have addressed the shortcomings that often limit the usefulness of evaluation research. They have tried to pay attention to the evaluation's end use—which means paying attention to users by involving them in the program evaluation process as valued stakeholders and framing questions to produce information that will relate directly to the choices that organizations must make regarding how to deliver their services.

One of the foremost members of the program evaluation profession, Michael Q. Patton, author of *Utilization-Focused Evaluation*, has urged evaluators to adopt a "utilization-focused" approach. By this, Patton means "evaluation done for and with specific, intended primary users for specific intended uses."[1]

As a result, thinking about program evaluation has shifted away from evaluation solely for accountability and toward evaluation approaches that emphasize the use of evaluation for improving and strengthening programs. (This does not imply less importance for accountability—just greater recognition of other, important purposes of program evaluation.)

This shift in thinking has resulted in increased recognition and appreciation of the importance of including program designers, managers, and funders in the process of program evaluation. Professional evaluators can support the process; they can develop and revise their work in ways that maximize the potential for use. Yet the ultimate decision to use evaluation results as a tool—both to improve service effectiveness and for other purposes—remains in the hands of those who must

---

[1] Michael Quinn Patton, *Utilization-Focused Evaluation* (Thousand Oaks, CA: Sage Publications, 1996), 23.

make program, service, and treatment decisions; those who allocate resources; and those who create policies.

So, the content of this book focuses on the *use* of program evaluation findings and is written for those involved in service delivery within nonprofit organizations: practitioners, designers, managers, funders, and others. Evaluation professionals and other researchers may find it very worthwhile as well, especially those who want to learn from programs, in their own words, about what makes evaluation useful and usable to them.

The Purpose and Development of This Book

This book offers illustrations of how organizations have used program evaluation research results. We emphasize, first and foremost, the use of evaluation for improving program and service effectiveness. That's primary. We move beyond program and service effectiveness, though, to illustrate the use of evaluation findings for other purposes: influencing policy and legislation and marketing (both to people outside of a program as well as to a program's own constituents such as board members and staff).

In developing this book, we contacted and completed interviews with leaders from forty different nonprofit organizations representing various fields including human services, community development, crime and safety, and education. Of the forty organizations, twelve are located in Minnesota and the others throughout the United States. All of the nonprofit leaders we interviewed had interesting stories and experiences with evaluation, but in a book of this nature, the sheer number can overwhelm. For this reason, we selected one in-depth example and fourteen other examples that illustrate the three primary uses of evaluation. All of the organizational profiles, and the ways they used evaluation, can be purchased. Visit the publisher's web site at http://www.FieldstoneAlliance.org.

We used a three-prong approach to identify examples of how organizations have used evaluation findings. We invited some of the organizations that we, at Wilder Research, have worked with to participate in interviews; we asked our network of local and national contacts to nominate organizations that might be good examples; and we looked through current publications and reports for the names of organizations that had done evaluations and had used the results. We decided to seek out examples, rather than conduct a random sample, and to describe evaluation use that might otherwise go unnoticed.

We took detailed notes during each of the interviews and created examples based on their answers. These we sent back to the organizations to be proofread and edited for accuracy. Then, we read these examples looking for themes of evaluation use. We found nine different types of use (for example, to improve programs and services, to influence policy and legislation, to increase revenue, to conduct public relations activities, and so on). These nine we divided into three primary uses (those that almost all the examples mentioned) and six secondary uses. We focus this volume on describing the three primary uses of evaluation, which include:

1. Improve programs and services

2. Influence policy and legislation

3. Market the organization

The book focuses on *real* examples and contains the ideas, suggestions, and actual words of people who you, the reader, would consider your nonprofit colleagues. We hope these stories stimulate and inspire you, and help you identify and create opportunities to use evaluation in many different ways for the benefit of the people your organization serves.

Before we turn to these stories, we cover some topics helpful for applying the experiences of other organizations to your own situation. First, we offer an overview of program evaluation. Then, we discuss use—what it means and what influences it.

Understanding Program Evaluation

TO APPRECIATE THE STRENGTH of program evaluation for specific uses, it is important to understand what the word *evaluation* means. It is also important to understand the features of a good-quality evaluation. So, in this chapter, we will review a definition of program evaluation, and we will look at some of the characteristics of evaluation. We provide references for readers who would like more details, including references to technical and nontechnical resources.

Evaluation—A Definition

Evaluation is a systematic process for an organization to obtain information on its activities, its impacts, and the effectiveness of its work, so that it can improve its activities and describe its accomplishments.

We take this definition from *The Manager's Guide to Program Evaluation* by Paul Mattessich.[2] The definition has several words of particular importance. As we now consider *the uses of evaluation findings* for program improvement and other purposes, some of those words deserve re-examination.

---

[2] Paul W. Mattessich, *The Manager's Guide to Program Evaluation* (Saint Paul, MN: Fieldstone Alliance, 2003).

As the definition states, program evaluation is "systematic." In other words, it is (or should be) designed in a way to ensure reliability, credibility, and usefulness.

> *Implications for promoting the use of evaluation findings:* Before anyone will use the findings from a program evaluation research study, they must trust the findings. If nobody believes the findings, they won't pay attention to them, and consequently, the findings will not have any effects. Systematically conducted evaluations produce results that people "buy into." This is a prerequisite for use.

Program evaluation is a process—not a onetime event but an ongoing set of activities to understand what an organization does and how it improves its activities over time. We'll say more about this later. For now, let's acknowledge that nothing about the typical nonprofit organization is static. The environment changes constantly, providing new opportunities and new challenges. Client volume ebbs and flows. Staff members come and go, perhaps too frequently. New ideas for providing service present themselves from time to time. Evaluation fits into this ongoing rhythm of organizational life.

> *Implications for promoting the use of evaluation findings:* We must understand that good evaluation research fits into a larger process of organizational design, assessment, and improvement. To make sure that we use evaluation research findings, we must build a process for use into our everyday routines.

Program evaluation offers "information." Evaluation bases itself on data. It provides information. Information is a raw resource, not something that, in and of itself, makes decisions or produces any other impact.

> *Implications for promoting the use of evaluation findings:* Information from an evaluation is available for us to craft into various forms for various uses.

Program evaluation is conducted "so that" something else can occur. In the *The Manager's Guide to Program Evaluation*, we noted that the ultimate goal of program evaluation is the use of information, either to better serve people or to represent an organization to others (which, in turn, can result in better service).

> *Implications for promoting the use of evaluation findings:* We should look for creative and productive ways to use evaluation results. Doing so will increase our ability to fulfill the missions of our organizations. We should also make sure that the design of all evaluations incorporates the input—including statements of intended uses—from intended users.

Above all, we need to recognize program evaluation as good, commonsense thinking. It extends the intuition and reasoning that we all do every day, whether at work or in our personal lives. If we want to make a sound decision about purchasing a major item like a car or an appliance, we know the worth of research to obtain the best quality and value. If we want to find the best route to travel to a location like work, school, or shopping—and several options exist—we know the worth of giving them all a try in order to compare them and discover which is the best. Truly, we all have "evaluation research competence," even if we don't realize it!

Program evaluation offers a tool that extends the reasonable, commonsense approaches to making decisions and solving problems. If you reach a point where evaluation seems too confusing or too complex to be useful, then you deserve to have it revised into a format that works for you. Some technical aspects of research may require special skills, for example the skills to do advanced statistical analysis, if called for in a specific evaluation. Similarly, some components of an automobile require the skills of a mechanic to understand (and repair!). However, nothing about the findings of evaluation research should keep users out of the driver's seat or impede their ability to drive.

Results-Oriented Evaluation Guides

This chapter mentions some of the features of program evaluation—not to attempt a thorough, detailed description but simply to provide a context for our later discussion of using evaluation results. Readers interested in more details should consult *The Manager's Guide to Program Evaluation* by Paul Mattessich, or take a look at one or more of the excellent evaluation references currently available.

The *Manager's Guide* provides a strategic, commonsense description of program evaluation. It describes the types of information that are critical for a valuable evaluation, and it identifies the strategic and operational questions that this information can answer. It also provides advice on whether and how to select consultants.

Most books on evaluation are oriented toward evaluation practitioners or professionals, rather than toward program managers, funders, and staff. If interested in more details, you might find the following helpful:

Mattessich, Paul W. *The Manager's Guide to Program Evaluation.* St. Paul, MN: Fieldstone Alliance, 2003. *Provides a manager's perspective on the phases of an evaluation study, the types of information to collect, and advice on selecting a research consultant.*

Patton, Michael Quinn. *Utilization-Focused Evaluation.* Thousand Oaks, CA: Sage Publications, 1996. *A classic. Provides both practical and theoretical insight related to identifying users, focusing an evaluation, selecting methods, analyzing data, and presenting findings.*

Rossi, Peter H., Mark W. Lipsey, and Howard E. Freeman. *Evaluation: A Systematic Approach,* 7th ed. Thousand Oaks, CA: Sage Publications, 2003. *Offers a technical, but readable and thorough, coverage of impact assessment, experimental design, and other methodological topics.*

York, Peter. *A Funder's Guide to Evaluation: Leveraging Evaluation to Improve Nonprofit Effectiveness.* St. Paul, MN: Fieldstone Alliance, 2005. *Discusses multiple ways that evaluation can be used by grantmakers and grantees to build capacity in leadership, adaptive capacity, management, and technical skills.*

Three Characteristics of Program Evaluation

As a potential user of program evaluation, it is worth knowing about three characteristics of evaluation:

- Evaluation as part of an ongoing process of program design, delivery, and improvement
- Stakeholder involvement
- Logic models

Evaluation as part of an ongoing process

We mentioned earlier that program evaluation is a process—not a one-time event but an ongoing set of activities. In fact, it fits into a larger process of program design, delivery, and improvement. In addition, it constitutes just one of several major influences (or potential influences) on decisions about what services to offer and how to offer them. Figure 1 illustrates this.[3]

Figure 1. Program Evaluation as Part of an Ongoing Cycle

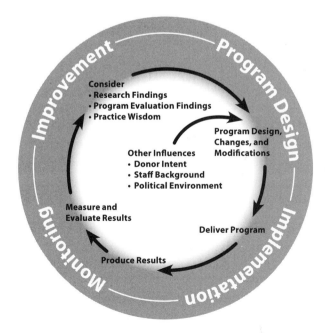

---

[3] Paul W. Mattessich, *The Manager's Guide to Program Evaluation* (Saint Paul, MN: Fieldstone Alliance, 2003), 10.

In looking at Figure 1, Program Evaluation as Part of an Ongoing Cycle, note that you could substitute the words "policy" or "funding allocation" for the word "program."

In a perfect world, decision making about what programs or services to offer and how to offer them would occur *after* we have the opportunity to review and digest reliable, succinct information. Staff of an organization would come together periodically, review the latest research knowledge, review the latest program evaluation findings on the effectiveness of their services to date, share their knowledge obtained through experience about the unique needs of the population they serve, and *then* draw conclusions and make decisions! Unfortunately such a reality does not exist, at least not yet, but the closer we can approach it the better our results will be.

Figure 1 offers, on the one hand, an ideal model for how evidence-based decision making can occur within the larger process of design and continuous improvement of programs. On the other hand, it reflects the reality that not all decisions will derive from a strict application of information, plus practice wisdom, plus logic.

The figure identifies four types of influences on program decisions: program evaluation findings, research findings, practice wisdom, and other influences. *Program evaluation findings* and their uses are, of course, the focus of this book. We will look at them extensively.

Research findings include, for example, studies of human behavior and studies of organizational behavior, as well as population studies describing the specific characteristics and needs of people within a specific region. These findings offer a general understanding of the need for programs or services and a general understanding of the types of effects that these programs or services might have.

Practice wisdom comes to professionals through their experience working with the individuals they serve.

Finally, *other influences* include such things as available resources, political considerations, staff training and background—items that we might not think of as part of the "rational model" for decision making, but which are, at least now, part of the process in our imperfect world.

It is important to understand that Figure 1 portrays an *ongoing* cycle. Doing, learning, and improving should all occur continuously for as long as an organization exists. Program evaluation is part of this, enabling an organization to know how it's doing and giving it the means to see whether options it pursues for improvement actually result in better results.

Stakeholder involvement

We mention this characteristic just briefly—but that does not imply any lack of importance. In fact, some people might consider stakeholder involvement as the single most critical ingredient for successful promotion of the use of program evaluation findings.

Among the first steps in evaluation—absolutely critical for success— is the identification of the intended users of the evaluation findings. Quoting Patton, we must focus on "intended uses for intended users."[4] Intended users are typically called *stakeholders*. Each stakeholder deserves, in a sense, to have some degree of "ownership" of the evaluation findings. Stakeholders need to be involved in planning an evaluation in order to maximize the likelihood that productive use of evaluation findings will occur. The seeds of use must be planted during the design phase of an evaluation, not after an evaluation has completed the collection and reporting of information.

To increase the chances that evaluation findings will be useful to you, the stakeholder, you should actively participate in evaluation design and identify others whose voice should be heard. This will create the greatest opportunity to have the evaluation provide information that is useful not only for program and service improvement but also for other purposes.

---

[4] Michael Quinn Patton, *Utilization-Focused Evaluation* (Thousand Oaks, CA: Sage Publications, 1996).

Logic models

Evaluation researchers and stakeholders have found it helpful to create logic models that illustrate how the activities of a program (or, you could use the words "services of a program" if that better suits you) lead to program outputs and eventually to the outcomes you want to achieve. Logic models portray your program's "theory."

A popular method for constructing logic models involves specifying inputs, activities, outputs, and outcomes. Outcomes are typically categorized as initial, intermediate, and longer-term. Figure 2, Logic Model, describes these components of logic models. Figure 3, Sample Logic Model, provides an actual example.[5]

Figure 2. Logic Model

Inputs	Activities	Outputs	Outcomes
Resources a program uses to carry out its activities, for example, staff, supplies, volunteers, money.	The actual work or services of a program. Things that staff and volunteers do, such as counseling, training, delivering meals, and other service delivery activities.	The accomplishments, products, or service units of a program, for example, the number of persons who received training.	Changes that occur in people, policies, or something else as a result of a program's activities.

Initial Outcomes: Changes that a program immediately produces in participants. For example, through training, a program might change people's knowledge, skills, or attitudes.

Intermediate Outcomes: Changes that occur later as a result of the initial outcomes. For example, people go to work as a result of knowledge and skills they gained.

Longer-term Outcomes: Changes that a program ultimately strives to accomplish and that follow from the intermediate outcomes. For example, as a result of going to work, people maintain a stable income and reside in decent housing.

---

[5] Paul W. Mattessich, *The Manager's Guide to Program Evaluation* (Saint Paul, MN: Fieldstone Alliance, 2003), 28–9.

Figure 3. Sample Logic Model

Logic Model: Teen Smoking Reduction Program

Program theory: Information and sustained support can enable teenaged persons to stop smoking. By providing a seminar and matching teens with a trained mentor, the program will change teen smoking behavior, with long-term positive consequences.

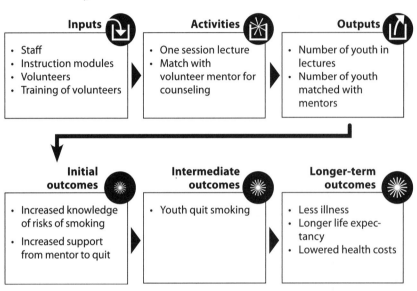

A logic model can alert you to information that is important to obtain in order to understand your program's effectiveness. It can also serve as a useful discussion piece and eventual reference point for staff because it represents visually, in one coherent diagram, the "beginning, middle, and end" of your organization's work. It brings together the thinking of your staff regarding the outcomes you hope to achieve through your work, and it helps get everyone to agree on the goals and outcomes.

Because of these characteristics, logic models often lead to increased use of evaluation findings. Logic models do this by providing a context for understanding what program evaluation information means and how it is associated with what you do. In addition, as mentioned above, logic models alert you to information that is important to obtain—not just during the initial design of an evaluation, but after a set of results has been produced and it is time to revise the evaluation in order to gather a new round of improved information.

Evaluators will typically bring together stakeholders to articulate their operating theory.[6] In the short run, stakeholders sometimes find this a painful process. We have worked with many organizations over the years that toiled over a precise statement of their mission, exact definitions of their services, or clear-cut statements of their intended outcomes. Believe it or not, some of the discussions generated by the need to state outcomes for program evaluation have led to major battles among the staff within an organization, or between staff and the evaluators of their program.

In one case, the staff of a program ceased communication with us for several months after we had initiated a discussion to clarify their outcomes. Then, they called and apologized. They assured us that we had done nothing wrong. Rather, we had prompted a discussion among the staff that forced them to be explicit about exactly what they wanted to accomplish. This led them to ask questions about who had responsibility for what within the different sections of their organization, and that discussion forced them to consider even more significant and sensitive topics related to "turf," organizational structure, supervision and management duties, and so on.

Nonetheless, in the long run, organizations find that the clear description of activities, outputs, and outcomes—as developed through the design of a program evaluation—provides many benefits. Some have even remarked that "getting us to articulate our mission and our goals was the most helpful thing the evaluators did for us." With a logic model, which describes your program's theory, you have a useful tool.

Before leaving this topic, one other point deserves mentioning. Ironically, the explosion in the use of logic models during the past ten years has sometimes made program evaluation more cumbersome and has even suppressed, rather than fostered, the use of evaluation for program improvement.

---

[6] See Michael Quinn Patton's *Utilization-Focused Evaluation* (Thousand Oaks, CA: Sage Publications, 1996) for a discussion of the "user-focused theory of action approach."

Why did this happen? Because rather than using logic models for simpli-fication, some organizations have attempted to make them into diagrams that capture *every* aspect and thought about their programs. Some logic models have so many boxes and arrows—occasionally arrows going in two directions or curving in odd, complex ways—that they become thor-oughly inscrutable. Perhaps you, yourself, have seen one of these!

Evaluation, in general, and logic models, in particular, should provide you with tools that simplify the complex reality of the world you work in. They should convey the many different aspects of your program in a coherent way. They should enable you and the audiences with whom you share the models to better understand what you do. They should increase understanding of the "cause and effect" chain that leads from what you do to beneficial outcomes for individuals, families, systems, communities, or even larger groups.

If your logic model fails to do this, then the tool is being misapplied. You need to step in and refocus the logic model to do what you need it to do.

Logic Model Resources

Readers who wish to know more about logic models may find the follow-ing resources helpful:

Measuring Program Outcomes: A Practical Approach by United Way of America, 1996. The United Way's well-known approach to logic models is included in this resource. Available from United Way at 703-212-6300.

W.K. Kellogg Foundation Logic Model Development Guide by Kellogg Foun-dation. This tool contains information on how to develop and ap-ply a program logic model. Available online at http://www.wkkf. org/Pubs/Tools/Evaluation/Pub3669.pdf

The Manager's Guide to Program Evaluation: Planning, Contracting, and Managing for Useful Results by Paul Mattessich, available from Fieldstone Alliance, www.FieldstoneAlliance.org, 800-274-6024.

Evaluation Results

What do you receive from an evaluation? Once a program evaluation has produced findings, what should you have? Let's respond to this at two levels:

First, program evaluation findings should provide you with four types of information: participant or client information, service data, documentation of results or outcomes, and perceptions about your services.

Second, program evaluation findings should enable you to answer strategic questions about your services.[7]

Four types of evaluation information

If done well, an evaluation should provide you with information that falls within four categories:

- Participant or client information. That is, information on who you serve, their characteristics, needs, and other attributes.

- Service data. That is, the type, volume, and other features of the services you provide or the activities you offer.

- Documentation of results or outcomes. That is, evidence of changes that have occurred; accomplishments that have been achieved; or needs that have been met among the people, families, groups, communities, or organizations that you serve.

- Perceptions about your services. That is, an indication of how people feel about what you do in general and about specific aspects of your activities.

---

[7] Here, we briefly describe these two items. For a more detailed explanation of the information that program evaluation should provide, along with a fuller description of the questions this information answers—by itself, as well as in combination with other information such as census data on your target population—see Chapter 2 of Paul W. Mattessich's *The Manager's Guide to Program Evaluation* (Saint Paul, MN: Fieldstone Alliance, 2003).

Ability to answer strategic questions about your services

With the information identified above, you can respond to questions such as

- What kinds of people do we serve and how many?
- Are these the people we have the intention or mission to serve?
- What services do people receive from our organization, or what activities do they take part in?
- Do certain types of people differ from one another in what they receive?
- What impacts do we have on the people, organizations, or communities we serve?
- How have our results been changing over time?
- What suggestions do service recipients have for improvement?

In addition, you can combine the information above with other available information such as census data, cost information, or comparable statistics from other programs, to respond to questions such as

- What proportion of our service or market area do we reach?
- How do we compare to similar organizations in numbers and types of people served?
- What is our cost per person or per unit of service?
- What does it cost to produce a successful "result"?

When you have credible answers to these questions, and many others, you will have a base from which you can work for program improvement, for influencing policy, for increasing revenue, for marketing your program, and for other uses of program evaluation.

Moving toward "Use"

In this chapter, we have set the stage for our discussion of use. We have defined what we mean by program evaluation, and we have identified some of its major features. We have described what a program evaluation should produce—in terms of general categories of information and in terms of strategic questions an evaluation can answer.

In the next chapter, we explore "use" a bit more before looking at real stories from real organizations that have put program evaluation findings to use for the benefit of themselves and the people they serve.

Using Program Evaluation Findings

BE HONEST. Why don't you make more use of applied research, specifically program evaluation? Or, if you find it uncomfortable to focus on yourself, think about people similar to you—those who design and manage programs, who deliver services, who set policy or allocate money. Why do you feel that they do not make more use of applied research, specifically program evaluation?

One answer is that in many situations, no current, relevant evaluation research findings exist, even when we have the strong desire to find and use them. However, that response diverts attention from acknowledging the importance of producing accurate evidence about our effectiveness and from using that evidence as part of an ongoing process of designing, monitoring, and improving policies, programs, and services.

A report from the Urban Institute stated

> Outcome data is often used to help measure effectiveness, and more nonprofits are involved in collecting this data each year. But it is still rare to find this valuable information being used to help improve the way services are delivered. Most often, it is reported to funders as a requirement under a grant and is put to little, if any, internal use by the organization. Many organizations do not appreciate or understand the potential usefulness of outcome information for improving services.[8]

---

[8] Urban Institute, "How and Why Nonprofits Use Outcome Information," Findings from a symposium (June 2002), http://www.urban.org/url.cfm?ID=310464

You, and others in similar positions, do have the ability to influence the use of evaluation, and you don't have to wait until after findings have become available in order to have this influence. You can have a hand in the development of evaluation findings by influencing what questions the evaluation will address, how it will address them, how information will be interpreted, and what formats the reports will have. As a result, you can shape the design of the work so the evaluation will produce findings that are beneficial to your organization for many different purposes. Not only *can* you do this, but you *must* if you want to ensure that your organization acts as effectively as possible both in meeting the needs of those you serve and also in marketing, informing, and educating current and new audiences.

Since this book has the goal to increase the use of evaluation information, we take some time to explore factors that influence that activity (or, as the Urban Institute would probably say, the factors that have led to *lack of use* in most organizations).

As the saying goes, it takes two to tango. Use of evaluation findings requires that both the evaluators and the potential users, or stakeholders, dance their parts. Janice Beyer, summarizing literature on why people use, or don't use, evaluation research findings noted a "cultural gap" between these two groups: "The most persistent observation in the literature on utilization is that researchers and users belong to separate communities with very different values and ideologies, and that these differences impede utilization."[9]

We have consulted the research literature about how people use evaluation research, and we have considered the experience we have gained over the years of work we have done with many different organizations. As a result of this search, we can suggest factors that influence the use of program evaluation findings by people in nonprofit organizations who could benefit from using them.

---

[9] Janice M. Beyer, "Research Utilization Bridging a Cultural Gap between Communities," *Journal of Management Inquiry* 6, no. 1 (1997): 17.

It's Not Just the User's Responsibility

Much evaluation research does not get used because, quite frankly, evaluation researchers have not created a useful, easily used product. While potential users of evaluation findings can encourage evaluators to take the steps necessary to make their products useful, primary responsibility for this falls on the shoulders of the evaluators. Evaluation researchers do, unfortunately, make some common mistakes that limit the value of their work. Typically, these relate to inadequate communication with, or involvement of, the intended users.

Much evaluation research does not get used because, quite frankly, evaluation researchers have not created a useful, easily used product.

Prevention of these mistakes requires that evaluation professionals incorporate at least the following ingredients into their work:

- Understanding of what decision makers need from evaluation
- Attention to intended uses by intended users (stakeholders)
- Strong, appropriate methodology
- Good communication, including good reporting

These factors relate to one another. For example, inadequate attention to intended uses by intended users will probably cause the evaluator to fail to understand the activities of decision makers and how evaluation information can assist those activities.

Understanding what decision makers need from evaluation

Sometimes evaluators fail to understand the activities of decision makers and how evaluation can help them. This may occur when evaluation researchers take an overly academic approach. Common complaints among organizations that have hired academic consultants are (a) that such consultants have their own agenda which dictated the questions addressed and the methods for addressing them, and (b) that academics fail to understand the realities of work in nonprofit and government service delivery organizations. However, evaluation consultants outside of academia can also fail to understand the realities of the organizations that hire them as well as the realities of other decision makers who could potentially use the evaluation findings.

Evaluation researchers have occasionally developed incomplete or unclear logic models, thus failing to incorporate a sound understanding of "program theory" into an evaluation. Because of this, evaluation results have missed significant features of service delivery and outcomes that are crucial to understanding both what a program achieved and why the program achieved it. Potential users feel the misfit between the evaluation and their program and, not surprisingly, dismiss the findings as irrelevant.

Sometimes, evaluators have not designed an evaluation that fits the decision-making time schedule of program designers, funders, or policymakers. Results, even if relevant and useful, arrive too late to be used.

To avoid these and similar problems, evaluators must take the time to understand how decisions are made and how evaluation fits into this process. They should understand what information needs to be gathered, on what timeline, and in what format. If they do, they will build into their work an understanding of the activities of decision makers and how evaluation fits into those activities.

Attention to intended uses by intended users (stakeholders)

Evaluation research, as implemented in many organizations, has not always involved stakeholders to the appropriate extent. In addition, even when stakeholders are consulted frequently—they have not always had the opportunity to state their information needs clearly and accurately. This happens, for example, when researchers do not take the time to check in with users about what they mean by certain words. It also happens when researchers do not coach and advise stakeholders about the types of information potentially available from an evaluation.

Evaluators must focus attention on intended uses by intended users. Typically, this requires frequent communication. Effective evaluators will probe for uses in several different ways, often on different occasions, after stakeholders have had time to think about the evaluation of their program and what it can produce for them. Often, while designing an evaluation, evaluators will do a "mock-up" of possible findings and show them to stakeholders. Occasionally, this helps stakeholders recognize that they need something different than they had originally thought in order to use the findings.

Strong, appropriate methodology

In some cases, evaluations have been flawed because they used a method that was not strong enough or was not well matched to the evaluation questions. For example, potential users who expected a credible, representative sample of a certain size, with figures they could cite as accurate measures, received instead some descriptive stories based on focus groups conducted with participants who could not be considered representative of any larger group. Or, potential users who hoped for detailed understanding of issues their clients faced regarding access to services and ways that they could improve their services in the eyes of consumers received data from a survey that related in only minor ways to the outcomes they sought and provided no detailed consumer feedback.

Evaluation often tackles some very tough measurement problems. Measuring change in the behavior of individuals, for example, can be very complex. Moreover, measuring change in organizations, systems, or communities is even more complex and challenging. Nonetheless, evaluation research that takes on the task of such measurement must do an adequate job. Otherwise, the results will fail to convince the audience.

Evaluators should have the competence to match methods to the questions users raise, so the information produced by the evaluation will relate directly to the users' needs. In addition, evaluators should implement whatever methods they select in ways that reasonable decision makers will consider strong and credible.

Good communication, including good reporting

Sometimes communication breakdowns occur during the course of evaluation research. When this happens, it typically results in a problem we already noted: failure to involve stakeholders to the appropriate extent. Other times, the problem is not so much that an evaluation has not gathered useful information; rather the reporting of that information has been weak. Perhaps it has been reported only in highly technical terms, or the report has been poorly written and edited.

Evaluators need to take steps to maintain constant communication with users during all phases of an evaluation. Obviously, user input during design is critical. However, such input is also very important after data have been collected and as data are being analyzed and interpreted. User input is also important as reports are being produced. Users can comment on the content of reports, and they can specify various formats that will effectively make the results available as a resource for all users whenever they need to consult them.[10]

This does not imply that users must understand every technical aspect of a program evaluation. But they should have no trouble understanding the findings. As one of the organizational representatives with whom we spoke for this book stated,

"On the front end, we are dumping in all kinds of numbers and statistics and information that do not seem to be related, and on the back end, they come out in a meaningful way that really tells the stories, that captures the essence of the program very well."

It's Not Just the Evaluator's Responsibility

Although evaluators probably bear most of the responsibility for making program evaluation useful and usable, they can only take potential users to the water—they can't make them drink. If you want to achieve

---

[10] Reading this, some may rightly ask: What about objectivity? Don't evaluators and users need to keep some distance, so reporting appears unbiased? Competent evaluators can maintain an objective position and, at the same time, integrate users into the design and reporting of evaluation research.

productive use of program evaluation findings for program improvement and other purposes, at least three ingredients are important to install within your organization:

- A culture open to innovation
- Realistic expectations about *what* program evaluation can do
- Realistic expectations about *how* program evaluation does what it does
- Creativity with respect to new uses of program evaluation information

A culture open to innovation

As evaluation has evolved during the past several decades, the significance of the decision maker's attitude and willingness to use research for decision making has remained evident.[11] Probably the most important factor that influences the likelihood that decision makers or stakeholders will use the findings produced by program evaluation is the existence of a culture open to new inputs. Heather Weiss, a well-known researcher and the director of the Harvard Family Research Project, asserted:

> Organizations with a culture that values inquiry, exploration, and discovery, as well as self-examination, are on the forefront of using evaluation to fine-tune their programs and be innovative. Where this 'culture of inquiry' is lacking, evaluators need to be prepared to adopt new roles as change agents who can dispel fears about evaluation and nurture change in an organization's mind-set.[12]

Stakeholders must adopt a mind-set open to making decisions based on information obtained through program evaluation. Stakeholders must also foster within their organizations a willingness to make

---

[11] Lipton cites earlier findings that the most important factor related to use of evaluation is "not the quality of the evaluation but the existence of a decision maker who wants and needs an evaluation and has committed himself to implementing its findings." Douglas Lipton, "How to Maximize Use of Evaluation Research by Policymakers." *Annals of the American Academy of Political and Social Science*, 521 (May 1992): 175–188.

[12] Heather Weiss, "From the Director's Desk," *The Evaluation Exchange* (Fall 2002): 1.

changes based on program evaluation findings. If an organization re-sists change, if staff members oppose any alteration of the status quo, then evaluation findings within that organization will not be used. Even if a few staff are open to change, they will need time and conscious ef-fort to overcome the resistance of their colleagues if a non-innovative culture has become entrenched in the organization.

Beyond being open to new ideas and willing to make changes, potential users must actually commit themselves to change and take concrete action—typically by building a process into their organizations that follows up on whatever the program evaluation discovers. As one of the organizational representatives we interviewed stated: "An evaluation only works if you're willing to listen to it. We had to very consciously take the chip off our shoulders. We had to be willing to listen."

Realistic expectations about what program evaluation can do

Productive use of evaluation findings requires that users have realistic expectations concerning what program evaluation can do. Practically speaking, users need to understand three things: 1) their work should combine efforts to do their current best with continuous improvement; 2) they should be prepared for the risk that evaluation will deliver in-formation that challenges their practices and beliefs; and 3) they must exercise good judgment with respect to the use of the information pro-vided by evaluation.

First, all of us see, or should see, our work as an ongoing effort to do as well as we can and to look continuously for ways to improve what we do. At any point in time, we will do what seems to be best—that is, what seems to have the greatest likelihood of success, the highest probability to achieve the outcomes we want to achieve with the people we serve. As time goes on, we learn new things and revise our thinking about what is "best." Program evaluation is part of our ongoing search for the best ways to do things.

Evaluation is *not* a technique that reveals the one and only effective way to do something. During the past decade or so, the identification of "best practices," often based on research evidence, has created the impression that perfect ways of doing things exist somewhere out there; we just have to discover them. As a result, some people conceive of program evaluation as the discovery mechanism for not yet visible "truths" or "laws." Some people even talk as if, with enough effort, we can discover immutable laws that will guide the way to deliver specific types of services, seemingly forever.

Instead, we need to view program evaluation similar to the way we look at any science. Science increases our knowledge. If done well, it increases the likelihood that we understand cause and effect; it increases our ability to predict the results of our actions. However, *scientific knowledge continually improves and revises itself*. Sometimes, new findings even contradict previous findings. As the Nobel Prize–winning physicist Richard Feynmann once said, "If the experiment produces a result in San Francisco, but it doesn't produce that result in Cleveland, then we can conclude that the experiment produced the result in San Francisco, but not in Cleveland." Though joking in a sense (since there's more to it than that), he wanted to emphasize that we should take in all the data we can in order to search constantly for new explanations and new ways of seeing the world. We need to retain even inconsistent data because, eventually, our understanding may reach a level where the inconsistent data can blend together in a way that makes sense.

Feynmann's comment pushes us to acknowledge that no one study will ever provide the be-all and end-all explanation of anything. Repeated studies of our own work and that of programs providing similar services to people of different types in different locations will enable us to make better decisions, to raise the probability that we will achieve our outcomes, and to contribute "scientifically" to understanding the best ways to deliver services.

A second thing related to realistic expectations about what program evaluation can do concerns the risk involved. A principal risk, of course, is that program evaluation may produce information that challenges a user's prior beliefs, conventional wisdom, or the predominant thinking within a field. And, as we all know, an evaluation may lead to negative political repercussions. There is no guarantee that evaluation findings will include something that pleases everyone. In fact, findings may displease everyone!

Third, judgment is still required. Evaluation produces information; it does not make decisions. Good evaluators will offer their interpretations, but such interpretations are simply additional information for decision makers. As Figure 1 in Chapter 1 indicated, decisions about what programs or services to offer and decisions about how to improve them, derive from a blend of evaluation, other research, practice wisdom, and so on. Users will want to incorporate credible evaluation findings into their decisions. With stronger findings, users will perhaps find decisions easier or less stressful. However, program evaluation will not supplant the user's decision-making role.

So, having realistic expectations about what program evaluation can do means

- Understanding that a single program evaluation may increase our knowledge and improve our ability to make decisions, but it won't provide the "ultimate" answers to questions about how best to design our programs and services.
- Being ready for bad news, unpleasant findings, or disappointing results.
- Recognizing that evaluation provides information; it does not make decisions. Users retain that responsibility.

Realistic expectations about how program evaluation does what it does

There are limits to evaluation—its scope, the time it takes, the resources required, and the roles of users and evaluators. These four items are discussed in greater detail in *The Manager's Guide to Program Evaluation*. Here, we just mention them briefly.

Scope refers to the limits governing the questions that program evaluation can answer. Simpler, more observable things are easier to measure than complex, less observable things. So, for example, you can count the number of people who receive your services more easily and accurately than you can measure their self-esteem—although both of these are possible.

Frequently, programs want to contribute to very long-term, positive outcomes for individuals or communities. In fact, they may justify their existence by suggesting that they will have effects long into the future, as in the example of a program that provides skills to elementary school children with the expectation that these skills will persist into their teenage and adult years, affecting their choices concerning relationships, citizenship, careers, and other significant activities throughout their lives. A program's logic model may include such long-term outcomes at the end of the diagram (with the label of "ultimate" or "long-term"). Practically speaking, it may not be possible to measure these outcomes, even if the program has the willingness and endurance to wait fifteen to twenty years for results. This does not mean that either the theory or the logic model is a poor one, nor does it mean that evaluation cannot occur. It only means that evaluation may only have the capacity to measure initial outcomes.

Program evaluation takes time, and results may take months or years to obtain. Much of this is obvious. For example, if you provide training with the intent that a participant will acquire knowledge or skills that they will apply during the following year, then you will have to wait a year before you know the extent to which you have achieved your outcome.

Resources matter for program evaluation. Many organizations that have attempted to do, or obtain, program evaluation at no cost have been disappointed. Even the simplest of evaluations require at least some time and effort on the part of an organization's staff. More complex evaluations require a lot of effort and may call for the hiring of an evaluation professional.

Finally, potential users of evaluation findings need to understand their own roles and the roles of evaluators within the program evaluation process. At every stage—design, data collection, analysis, and reporting—users have important tasks to carry out. If they fail to accomplish these tasks, they reduce the likelihood that the evaluation will provide as many useful and usable findings as it potentially could.

So, having realistic expectations about how program evaluation does what it does means recognizing the issues of scope, time, resources, and roles.

Creativity with respect to new uses of program evaluation information

Earlier, we mentioned the importance of having a culture open to innovation in order to maximize the likelihood that program evaluation findings will be used to improve programs. Indeed, the primary reason for doing program evaluation is, and probably will always be, to obtain information on a program's activities and accomplishments in order to improve the effectiveness of the program.

However, since our goal is to help you to think about ways you can use program evaluation findings not only for program improvement but also for other purposes, it is important to mention the significance of creative uses of program evaluation information. This involves developing awareness among staff of additional ways to use program evaluation findings—for example, to influence policy, to promote the organization, or to educate consumers. It also involves establishing organizational expectations that encourage suggestions and experimenting with new uses. At present, using program evaluation findings for purposes other than program improvement is uncharted territory. That's why this book includes illustrations of innovative ways that organizations are using evaluation.

Uses of Evaluation

Patton identifies "intended use by intended users" as the primary focus of program evaluation.[13] In his writing and in his work with organizations, he has devoted significant attention to encouraging the use of evaluation. After all, if we don't intend to use it, why should we do it?

By the word *use*, most people mean applying evaluation findings to decisions about services or products that an organization provides. In other words, people use evaluation to improve the effectiveness of services and products.

This book contains examples of this type of use. However, evaluation results can help an organization to improve its performance in other ways as well. Later in this book, we illustrate these forms of use by providing many examples of them. Here, we offer some brief definitions of three primary uses of evaluation: 1) to improve service quality, 2) to influence policy and legislation, and 3) to market the program. Note that from an individual organization's perspective, there may be more uses; we've collapsed them here for simplicity. In particular, other "uses" or benefits of improving service quality, influencing policy and legislation, and marketing programs include: increasing revenue, generating positive public relations, influencing grantmakers' decisions and financial policies, increasing staff morale and motivation, and project management.

1. Improve service quality

The diagram we saw earlier (Figure 1, page 13) illustrates this use. Most commonly, we use evaluation findings to understand how well we have done, to identify ways to improve, and then to measure again to see if we have actually improved. Program evaluation offers measures of effectiveness. It enables us to understand our overall outcomes and certain aspects and nuances of these outcomes. For example, evaluation can tell us the extent to which our program meets the needs of all the people we serve, and it can indicate whether we meet more needs of

---

[13] Michael Quinn Patton, *Utilization-Focused Evaluation* (Thousand Oaks, CA: Sage Publications, 1996) 20.

certain groups (men or women, elderly or youth). Use of evaluation findings for program and service improvement means applying evaluation findings to decisions about programs and services, either as the most significant input or one of several inputs.

In addition to using evaluation findings to directly improve programs and services, other secondary uses of evaluation also support program and service improvement. Evaluation findings can be used to understand program activities and how those activities conform to a plan, with the intention to make mid-course corrections as appropriate. Evaluation findings can also be used to improve staff morale and motivation; high staff motivation and morale support the primary work of using evaluation findings to improve service and program quality.

2. Influence policy and legislation

Evaluation findings, such as program outcomes, can be communicated to policymakers to influence policy and legislative decisions. Policymakers belong to funding organizations or local, regional, and national legislative bodies. Use of evaluation findings to influence policy and legislation often means involving policymakers on evaluation consultative committees, and working to communicate the findings in appropriate language that policymakers can understand. When successful, evaluation findings can influence how and to whom funders allocate grants, what services they support within a geographical area, or which service sector (for example, youth development, education, or health) they identify as highest priority for their attention.

3. Market the organization

Use of evaluation findings for marketing means communicating to potential clients, consumers, or donors about the results of an organization's services to influence more people to use and fund those services. Benefits of using evaluation findings to market the organization can include increased revenue, positive public relations, consumer education, and increased staff morale and motivation.

Summary

In this chapter, we have discussed issues related to promoting use of evaluation findings. We saw that most organizations do not make maximum use of evaluation findings, and we identified some ways that organizations can increase their use.

Now, we will move on to examine specific examples of how organizations have used evaluation findings, both for improving their work and for other important purposes.

How YouthZone
Maximizes Evaluation

IN THIS CHAPTER AND THE NEXT, we take a look at examples of how nonprofit organizations around the United States have used program evaluation findings for program and service improvement and other purposes. The chapters emphasize a "peer-to-peer" approach—attempting to provide you, the reader, with close-to-firsthand glimpses of real cases from real organizations.

Reflecting on the forty organizations with whom we visited, we have many, admirable illustrations of exciting, creative work. For example,

- Allies Against Asthma, in Seattle, Washington, used evaluation to improve its service to families. It also used evaluation findings to improve its bylaws and develop public relations activities.

- Taller San Jose, in Santa Ana, California, found that in addition to increasing the quality of its work with gangs, evaluation greatly increased its credibility with funders.

- Minnesota Family Investment Program used evaluation not only to improve its organization's services and conduct a public relations campaign, but also to successfully influence state welfare policy by illustrating the diverse population of people using welfare services.

- The Bridge of Northeast Florida, in Jacksonville, used evaluation research to raise awareness about youth issues and to increase revenue. The organization distributed a marketing letter to the community and used annual reports and grant proposals as methods to increase visibility and to raise funds. Evaluation results were included in all these documents to show evidence of the organization's success.

We decided to select one of the forty for an in-depth look at how a nonprofit organization can put evaluation research to many worthwhile uses. YouthZone, in Colorado, used the results of their evaluation research for every purpose we had in mind, and even more. So, we share with you what we learned from our conversations with Debbie Wilde, the executive director of YouthZone, about how she and her staff put evaluation research to use.

YouthZone Intervention Services

Debbie Wilde looks very enthusiastically at what evaluation has done for her organization: "As an executive director, I am so glad that I had a backup for my stories about what our program does. It's given us another dimension. Lots of programs have touchy-feely stories. We have those too, and we do good work, just like other programs. But I can tell you what we do and what impacts it has in the scientific language of this business, and this ability has given me more confidence in being bold about talking with people who have financial resources, in doing public relations, and in being assertive in asking for referrals. I feel like I really have solid ground to stand on. Not just me but my board as well. It's really given us confidence in our organization."

YouthZone serves youth ages six to eighteen and their families. It delivers counseling, mentoring, life-skills education, court services, and other forms of prevention and intervention services. YouthZone provides services within two and a half counties on the western side of Colorado, including Glenwood Springs, a portion of the Colorado River valley, and the Aspen area. Started in 1976, the organization has the overall mission to promote the development of young people as responsible and contributing citizens.

**Specific Changes YouthZone Made
as a Result of Its Evaluation**

- Added exit interviews with parents when participants complete
the program

- Began identifying high-risk kids when they enter the program and
doubled the number of supervisors who look at these kids

- Changed staff qualification requirements

- Changed programming to ensure kids stay connected to schools,
families, and communities

- Created talking points that illustrated the program's impact for
board and staff to use in fundraising efforts

- Tailored evaluation data to communicate the program's value to
different audiences—criminal justice agencies, organizations working with youth, county and city governments, and so on—to keep
referrals coming

Intervention Services, a project of the YouthZone organization, has
goals to reduce delinquency, reduce substance abuse and use, improve
self-concept, increase decision-making skills, and increase pro-social
development. Intervention Services focuses on youth who have exhib-
ited drug-use behaviors. As part of its effort to increase pro-social development, the program strives to keep youth connected to schools,
families, and communities.

According to Wilde, three major motivations lay behind YouthZone's
decision to conduct an evaluation of Intervention Services:

1. Staff wanted to answer the question, "Are we making a difference?" They wanted to document and understand how much of
an impact they could really have with youth.

2. For motivation purposes, staff wanted to validate that what they
did truly had value in the lives of youth.

3. Staff sought to increase opportunities for funding and felt that
objective, credible information about the effectiveness of their
program could assist them in doing this.

Evaluators outside of the organization have done the evaluation work, which occurs on a three-year cycle.

The following pages contain questions and answers about YouthZone's evaluation of its Intervention Services program.

Q: *How did you use the evaluation to improve the effectiveness of your programs or services?*

A: Each time we did the evaluation, particularly the first time, we followed up on the recommendations. And, really, the follow-up was the telling tale. The first evaluation included a list of recommendations from the evaluators. We took that list, methodically reviewed the recommendations, and tried to see what makes sense—can we do these changes? We then followed through with some changes.

By putting all the data in context, we were able to begin to identify the "high-risk" kids. We had a huge sample—764 in the second evaluation and even larger in the first one. We could identify a high-risk category of kids. Then, we were able to focus on particular items that we would always pay attention to when a kid comes in. The tools that grew from the evaluation gave us a really clear initial assessment—just a glance— really zeroing in much quicker on assessment issues.

The evaluation helped us recognize some things about staffing—what kinds of people we needed. As a nonprofit—what sorts of kids are we working with? If we have these kinds of kids, then what staff qualifications do we need?

We had noticed that some students left our program with a higher risk score or with not much improvement. Part of what we identified through the evaluation is that kids aren't done when they finish our program. We pay attention to the word "exit." To achieve the outcomes we want to have for the kids, the best thing to do is have an exit interview with parents. At the exit interview, we explain to the parent how we're still concerned about: a, b, and c with their child. Or, maybe we can say, "hurray"—the kid is improving through the program. This all really changed in the programming after the first evaluation.

We also learned to give better attention to the high-risk kids—doubling the number of supervisors to look at the high-risk kids. We make sure we have a couple of people looking at those kids and what is going on.

Another very important thing came out of the evaluation—looking at drugs and alcohol—we saw that education was most effective. We found no correlation to change related to anything about public service. So, we changed the "youth public service" part of our program—to see how that would measure. After we made some changes, we saw big improvement—really affecting the things kids had control over. In the same way, related to self-concept and pro-social development, we changed our programming a little bit to focus more on family, school, and community. We really stressed: Are the kids connected with them? On the second evaluation we saw significant improvement.

Q: *How did you use the evaluation to increase revenue?*

A: From the evaluation, we made talking points for our board and staff. We were able to say "Here, we should look at this: kids aren't re-offending again." We were able to use that—"Here's the significant impact that we've made." We did it in lots of different ways, in meetings with local government, private donors, and foundations. It's a huge piece in the competitiveness of trying to get financial resources.

The evaluation was really helpful with getting funding
from local governments, the local system.
We could say "You should fund us. See the impact.
Help us keep serving kids."

The evaluation was really helpful with getting funding from local governments, the local system. We could say "You should fund us. See the impact. Help us keep serving kids." When the rubber meets the road, it's the dollar. When things are tight people want to know about results. What is my dollar getting me? That's where we really use evaluation heavily.

Q: *What about public relations and marketing?*

A: We have used the evaluation to tell our story—who we are and that we're effective. We are not just good programming. There is an end to this problem that we're addressing.

Q: *How did you use the evaluation to increase referrals?*

A: All of what we've already talked about affected the increase in referrals. We took information from the evaluation and aimed it at different areas: criminal justice agencies, organizations working with youth, county government, towns, and so on. These different audiences are trying to keep dollars down. We wanted to keep these referrals, and we used pieces of the evaluation with different audiences.

We were able to speak with these audiences, using objective information. We could document what was happening with kids, point to the barriers and ways to overcome them, and show that the success of kids in schools was having an impact on other areas of their lives.

We used the evaluation to encourage more partnering—to see if we could work with more kids and have a much better impact.

Having the numbers, showing that things are effective, getting more kids involved, seeing the positive outcomes—this provides accountability, legitimacy. It let us have a sense that important things are happening—that there are outcomes, and that there is impact.

Q: *When the evaluation was originally designed, did you intend to use it the way you did?*

A: Yes, for sure, for financial resources and for program improvement, and then I think we found even more things. We learned more and more things—which beget other program improvements we thought about. It's been fun. It gave us a different, new angle.

For example, the Rotary Club—it's really hard to get in to do a presentation. But we had another angle. We were not just another nonprofit; we could report on our evaluation. We could do a "profile of youth" in the valley. Because the sample is so large—with such a statistically valid instrument—we had a great analysis. We could apply it to a million things there. It really gave me an avenue to talk about what we're doing at YouthZone, but I can also discuss what the kids look like in the area. I can give a multi-service profile of the youth. This also gave me a whole different angle for several newspaper and radio stories as well.

It also helped us evaluate cost. We don't want to put a lot of energy into something that isn't effective—or cost effective. We weren't originally thinking about this going in.

Q: *Did you experience any barriers to utilizing the results? If so, how were the barriers overcome? What advice would you give to staff of other programs facing such barriers?*

A: Initially, we had a major barrier getting the staff to believe that this instrument was useful and that we were getting reliable information. They weren't interested. There's still some stuff going on. For staff to be evaluated, that's a huge barrier. There is resistance from those taking a close look at themselves. Staff are scared of what they might find out.

But then, when the evaluation came back and it showed we're making a significant difference—then staff said "hey, this is a good tool."

"My advice, as a director, is that it's really important to have trust in the evaluation and to believe it will give a valuable return. Ask staff to focus on it."

Any evaluation needs to address staff concerns. My advice, as a director, is that it's really important to have trust in the evaluation and to believe it will give a valuable return. Ask staff to focus on it. One of the biggest pieces for a nonprofit is truly being invested in your mission. Then ask honestly, "Don't we really want to know we are making a difference?" Don't be afraid to change if you need to in order to do a better job meeting the mission. Outside people respond to evaluation—they see that you're really focusing on this.

Cost was also a barrier. It's a lot of money—over a three-year period—even just doing it once every three years.

Q: *Approximately, how much did the evaluation cost?*

A: Ten thousand dollars. A hit of $10,000 in one program year is a big hit. We take it seriously—we have to have resources set aside for this. We need to continue this; it's too important to drop it. It's really become a part of how we do business as opposed to an afterthought. I know that some nonprofits have the attitude, "Let's get this done and put it on the shelf." But for us, it's almost a constant tool that we're using. I pull the evaluation out—at least parts of it—daily. We use it constantly in planning and programming. We use the assessment tools on a regular basis—inputting data, using data—all this turns into data collection for the evaluation. We measure before and after. The end result of all this input becomes an evaluation after three years. Then we have an annual report with running data. We take all the demographic data, and we take the outcome information from pre- and posttests. Then, we lay these over each other. The evaluation needs to be valuable to us in order to justify paying that kind of money. Otherwise, it seems foolish to do all that data collection.

Q: *What advice would you give to other programs hoping to utilize their results in similar ways?*

A: Do it. Make it a part of how you do business. Make it a part of how you operate. Just like I said before, it becomes a significant piece of your standard operating procedure. Then you feel like you truly get the return from it. The value of it is so clear to you.

My other advice: Don't be afraid of it!

Q: *What was the most important thing you learned about using evaluation results?*

A: How valuable the evaluation is—and how powerful it is. Also, how to make it work *for* us—how to use it. That has been a discovery process. Some of those things are now standard operating procedure. For example, I started doing a quarterly letter to colleagues for referral sources, giving them information from the evaluation—demographics and other things.

Evaluation changed how we do business in a lot of ways. It's really important for the board of directors. It has made the story of the organization so much more solid. Their buy-in is so much stronger. People can really get on board with making a difference. That's what I see.

Q: *Looking back on the evaluation, are there things you wish that you had done differently to make the results more useful?*

A: I haven't come up with anything. It's pretty thorough.

Q: *Is there anything else you would like to add, that you think might help your colleagues in other nonprofit organizations?*

A: What started as our evaluation has become "research" for us, in a sense. A researcher who does lots of social research on violence prevention, etc., has really gotten interested in what we do. She says, "You're the functional piece of all this research. You have the components for improving the lives of youth."

With our evaluation, we could really relate to her. The evaluation has driven the development of some of those components, such as the exit interview and identifying a high-risk kid. Some of these have become a part of our program and the way it functions.

We did the first evaluation, and we *used* the recommendations. We used them seriously. Then, we saw increased improvement in the second evaluation. We saw significant differences later. There was clear improvement in the results we were seeing from the first three years and the second three years.

So, I would advise other nonprofits to *follow* the recommendations. Strive for the best programming. Promote excellence. Promote knowing what you're doing—not being afraid of being accountable. Don't be afraid to stop funding mediocre programs.

Spend money on evaluation, so you can use it.

Keep in mind the positives evaluation can have for staff morale. Evaluation attracts good people to your board and good people to volunteer with your program. It communicates that this is the kind of program people want to be a part of—as staff or as volunteers.

"Evaluation attracts good people to your board and good people to volunteer with your program. It communicates that this is the kind of program people want to be a part of—as staff or as volunteers."

Summary

In this chapter we provided an in-depth example of how YouthZone used evaluation findings. This example illuminates how evaluation findings were used to improve programs and services, to increase revenue, to promote and market the organization, and to increase referrals. The next chapter focuses specifically on the three primary uses of evaluation: improving programs and services, influencing policy and legislation, and marketing services. We provide several organizational examples to describe how programs have used evaluation in these ways.

Promising Uses among Forward-Thinking Organizations

IN THIS CHAPTER, WE TAKE A LOOK at how specific nonprofit organizations around the United States have used program evaluation findings. We take a "peer-to-peer" approach, presenting this information, as much as possible, in the words of the people we interviewed—with the hope that their stories inspire you with real lessons from real organizations.

There are three major sections in this chapter. Each section is devoted to one of the primary uses of evaluation we've identified—to improve service quality, to influence policy and legislation, and to market services. Within each of these sections, we present examples drawn from our interviews. Each example briefly describes a program, identifies how the program conducts evaluation, illustrates how the program used evaluation findings, and provides other "words of wisdom" regarding what the program learned from its experience, what it would do differently, and what advice it has for others.

Finally, each of these sections includes suggestions if you want to use evaluation findings in a similar way.

Using Evaluation Results to Improve Service Quality

Most commonly, we use evaluation findings to understand how well our services have achieved what we want them to achieve, to identify ways to improve, and then to measure again to see if we have actually improved.

Program evaluation offers *measures* (note the plural—not just "one measure") of effectiveness. It enables us to understand our overall outcomes. It also enables us to understand certain aspects and nuances of these overall outcomes. So, for example, evaluation can tell us the extent to which our program meets the needs of all the people we serve, and it can indicate whether we meet more needs of certain groups (men or women, elderly or youth).

Use of evaluation findings for program and service improvement means applying evaluation findings to decisions about programs and services, either as the most significant input or as one of several inputs.

In the following examples, two domestic violence programs, an adult and family crisis support program, an oral health program, and a youth delinquency prevention program describe how they use program evaluation for service improvement. The first example describes how program evaluation provides a base for ongoing quality improvement and how evaluation supports innovation. The second example focuses on a specific decision an organization made to add new services in order to meet the needs of a group for whom traditional services were not effective. The third example describes how one organization uses evaluation for ongoing monitoring of its program effectiveness and a specific decision they made to add a new service. The fourth example highlights how evaluation was used to address particular challenges of the organization. Finally, the last example describes the challenges of using evaluation findings to improve program and service when there is resistance.

Domestic Abuse Project Therapy Program

▶ Improve Service Quality
Influence Policy and Legislation
Market a Program

Program

The Domestic Abuse Project (DAP), located in Minneapolis, Minnesota, began its Therapy Program in 1979 as the first domestic violence therapy program in Minnesota. This program provides services to meet the needs of women, men, children, and adolescents dealing with domestic violence. The overall goal of the Therapy Program is to ensure that victims of domestic violence can move beyond their experiences and live the rest of their lives in a safe household environment.

Evaluation

Shortly after the program started, DAP began program evaluation to demonstrate to funders and program staff the effectiveness of the program and to determine ways to improve. The Therapy Program has consistently evaluated its outcomes through follow-up studies. Clients who complete the program are evaluated six months after they exit the program to determine whether the Therapy Program was successful. Evaluation, including interviews with the victims, determines whether or not violence has stopped.

Evaluation use—Improve service quality

Through the evaluation, Therapy Program staff members learn whether program services enable clients and their families to protect themselves from future domestic violence. DAP uses evaluation to improve the quality of existing programs; it also uses evaluation to provide direction for new programs. Often, open-ended comments provide insight that enables the Therapy Program to better tailor its services to meet the needs of diverse clients.

For example, after learning that women needed more support services after leaving their Therapy Program group, DAP established an aftercare group for women in need of additional support services in groups with others experiencing similar issues around domestic violence. Importantly, after making a change, DAP monitors closely to see whether that change has actually resulted in an improvement and to make sure it has had no negative consequences.

"We are called the Domestic Abuse Project, and we take that name seriously. We take feedback from clients, pieces from new models, and we try them out to see if they will enhance our work. We do not want to compromise our outcomes, so we keep the same evaluation tools as we change our programs. After implementing a new idea, we ask ourselves if our outcomes change for the better, worse, or not at all. This evaluation process has allowed us to innovate over time. We have been able to compare and contrast outcomes over time."

The Domestic Abuse Project incorporates evaluation into an ongoing cycle of program design, operation, and improvement. It provides Therapy Program staff with timely feedback from the program evaluation. Every quarter, the program reviews the evaluation results at their all-staff meeting. In the meeting, they discuss the overall program goals and whether or not those goals were met. The open-ended comments shared with staff are particularly valuable, motivating them with the success stories of their clients. Staff also use evaluation to try new things—envisioning ideas, implementing those ideas, and evaluating their outcomes to make sure changes work.

According to the program's executive director, evaluation has motivated staff to develop professionally. "Evaluation and research has served as a growth piece for our professional staff here at DAP as they have worked with our evaluator to learn more about the process and, at times, co-publish articles about our work. Staff would not have had the same opportunities for growth if we were not open to evaluation. We have a culture here that is committed to evaluation, research, and learning, and making it a staff development piece as well.

Questions and answers

Q: *What barriers have you experienced in using evaluation results, and how did you overcome those barriers?*

A: The biggest barrier that we have had is implementation, being consistent with the model. When you are a nonprofit organization, you are subject to costs all the time. Keeping evaluation a high priority because it is time consuming and costs money may be difficult. When we lost a grant that paid for this evaluation work, we had to scramble internally to say that this is important to continue even though we have to bear the full cost of it. We have to monitor the quality of the evaluation tool and make sure it is implemented consistently. If it is done incorrectly, the results can compromise the outcomes. It takes a real commitment to make sure the data are accurate. That's the biggest barrier—the commitment to the resources to implement evaluation in an ongoing way.

Q: *What advice do you have for programs hoping to use their evaluation results in similar ways?*

A: It is critical to work with someone who knows how to do evaluation research. Our evaluator has been helpful to us, creating a reliable tool. I feel confident reporting the results because I know they are accurate. We use the most stringent measure possible, and we interview the partners of the men in our program. Some domestic violence programs rely on interviewing men or on police re-arrest data, which are not as reliable. We learned this by working with an evaluation consultant who understood our field, our program, and our research and evaluation needs.

Make a commitment. Evaluation is just as important as any other part of the program. There are limited resources, and you need to do the best work possible with the resources you have. The only way you will know you are providing those services is if you do regular evaluation to make sure you are effective. Evaluation is part of doing the business.

Q: *What is the most important thing you have learned through your evaluation activities?*

A: We learned how to interpret evaluation findings and outcomes. Now, when reading about another program's research and evaluation, we know whether or not the results are telling us something valuable. We can also examine the tools used by another evaluator and ask meaningful questions to determine whether or not the research is valid, or if an outcome measure is off base. A tool may not be effective, as we have learned through our evaluation work.

Q: *Anything else?*

A: We believe that we benefit the researchers as well. They do better research as a result of *partnering* with social service organizations. We protect the clients we work with because we question the safety of the researchers' work. We also help researchers with creation of evaluation outcomes and with interpretation of the outcome results. Direct service providers frequently see things in a different light compared to researchers. We know how to work with clients, what questions to ask, and how often to ask them. We have had researchers who want to work with battered women without being sensitive to the language and issues women experiencing domestic violence face. For starters, women in our organization do not always identify themselves as "battered" women. You have better research, better questions, and better outcomes as a result of researchers partnering with direct service providers. They work together to develop useful questions and meaningful outcomes.

Men's Domestic Abuse Program	▶ Improve Service Quality
	Influence Policy and Legislation
	Market a Program

Program

The Men's Domestic Abuse Program, operated by the Amherst H. Wilder Foundation in St. Paul, Minnesota, intends to reduce and eliminate violent and abusive behavior among men with a history of domestic abuse or assault. The program serves men from a variety of socioeconomic and ethnic backgrounds who are court ordered to attend. During weekly counseling and educational groups, staff work to provide a positive counseling experience for clients and encourage them to take responsibility for their behavior.

Evaluation

Through follow-up interviews with clients and their partners, research staff assess satisfaction with the Men's Domestic Abuse Program and measure its effectiveness in reducing violence. Follow-up measurement includes use of a Conflicts Tactics Scale, which ascertains the extent of verbal, emotional, physical, and sexual abuse that might be occurring. In addition, the follow-up explores adjustments in housing, employment, and social contacts for the clients. An annual program evaluation report presents the findings.

Evaluation use—Improve service quality

On the whole, results from this evaluation have been positive; men from all ethnic backgrounds report high levels of satisfaction with the services they receive. However, during the program's early years, staff who served as leaders of the counseling and education groups suspected that African American men were leaving the program at a higher rate than men from other ethnic backgrounds.

Several years after the launch of the evaluation, these staff concerns prompted a closer analysis of existing research data trends in the program. Special attention was paid to ethnicity-based variations in the data. The results of this analysis confirmed the staff's perceptions. Completion rates for African American men were consistently more than 20 percent lower than completion rates for clients from other ethnic backgrounds. This disparity was troubling, especially since African American men make up a large percentage of the clients served by the program.

In response to these findings, the Men's Domestic Abuse Program developed a separate, ethnically homogeneous counseling group for African American men. The group is led by an African American facilitator and supplements the standard program content with culturally specific materials on topics such as racism and oppression. Fittingly, the evaluation that first alerted staff to the need for an African American men's group has since attested to its success. In the program's most recent evaluation report, the completion rate for African American men was nearly equal to the rate for men from other ethnic backgrounds.

According to the program director, clients served in the African American men's group say they feel comfortable and understood within the group. "This feels so good for the men," he explained, "because they say this is their first experience where they're walking into a room full of black men, a black facilitator, and they don't have to worry about all that other stuff."

Questions and answers

Q: *What barriers have you experienced in using evaluation results, and how did you overcome those barriers?*

A: Unfortunately, sometimes there were time constraints involved when probation officers were trying to get their clients into the African American Men's Group. Since we were only offering one session of the African American Men's Group at a time (starting and ending with the same group of people), there may have been a waiting period. The probation officers felt pressured to get a client into a group immediately, so the client could complete the group before his probation period expired. Understandably, even though the probation officers knew their clients would be better served in the African American Men's Group, they would refer them to the heterogeneous group instead. This was not always a good solution because the chances that an African American man would successfully complete the heterogeneous group were far less. So, it is not only important that we pay attention to the research results, but also that we get the attention of the referral sources and collaborating partners as well.

Q: *What advice do you have for programs hoping to use their evaluation results in similar ways?*

A: If you're collecting data like we were, pay attention and act on it. Our discovery was somewhat of a coincidence. We could have acted on it much sooner if we had been more attentive to what the data was telling us.

Common Ground Sanctuary

▶ Improve Service Quality
Influence Policy and Legislation
Market a Program

Program

Located in Oakland County, Michigan, Common Ground Sanctuary helps adults and families in crisis by providing psychiatric emergency services, community intervention services, transitional living programs, a twenty-four-hour crisis hotline, and in-home crisis counseling. The program, which has been operating since 1970, serves approximately

27,000 people per year through its hotline services alone. While certain program areas target youth or adults more specifically, Common Ground Sanctuary serves all people experiencing a crisis.

Evaluation

All Common Ground Sanctuary programs are evaluated on an ongoing basis with results reported every quarter. These evaluations serve as quality improvement measures for the organization. While most evaluation work is done internally, the organization works with external evaluators when appropriate. Common Ground Sanctuary opted to develop these ongoing program evaluations to show community funders and the general public the success of its organization.

Evaluation use—Improve service quality

One goal of Common Ground Sanctuary is to assign a disposition to an individual within three hours after that person's enrollment in the psychiatric program. Measured on a monthly basis, the program hopes to accomplish this goal 95 percent of the time. If staff members realize they are not meeting the goal, they consider what is wrong with the current process and make necessary changes. For Common Ground Sanctuary, assigning dispositions is important because dispositions help measure the outcome of whether people feel better about their life situation after receiving counseling services.

Common Ground Sanctuary also examined its street outreach program and determined that it was not reaching enough kids. After looking at internal evaluation results and the work of other organizations, Common Ground Sanctuary recognized the need for a drop-in center to supplement their street outreach program. Both their data and other evaluation data showed that organizations can better reach youth after developing relationships through a drop-in center model. According to the organization's director, "Using evaluation data helps us get the funding that we need. After developing the drop-in center, if we do not find successful outcomes for youth, then we may drop the entire street outreach program."

Common Ground Sanctuary's use of evaluation to improve programs and services had an additional benefit of motivating staff. "When staff are involved with quality improvement work, they set standards for themselves and they meet them. Then, they feel really good about their work. It is important to set real objectives about what you are trying to accomplish. Even our board gets excited if they see that we have missed a target and then see us reach that same target later. This shows the board that we are telling the truth about our work. When we improve our services based on evaluation data and essential changes indicated by the data, it is a good morale booster for staff and board."

Questions and answers

Q: *What barriers did you experience in using evaluation results, and how did you overcome these barriers?*

A: One barrier is fear of what the results might show, which could be threatening to some people. To address this fear, you have to demonstrate to staff that there is no penalty if evaluation results are negative. You are using the results to make things better for the organization, not to upset staff. It is critical to keep evaluation separate from performance review. You also have to find a way to make evaluation a regular part of someone's job. Otherwise, it will not be taken seriously and you will get inaccurate or incomplete data.

Q: *What advice do you have for programs that hope to use their evaluation results in similar ways?*

A: Allocate serious resources to make sure evaluation happens. Someone has to be the driver of evaluation within the organization. Also, make sure your evaluation is nonthreatening to staff.

Q: *What is the most important thing you have learned through your evaluation activities?*

A: The most important thing that I have learned is that there are intangible positives that come from evaluation. Our agency has a high self-esteem about itself because we know what we are doing is working and when it doesn't work, we know what we can do to change things.

There is a certain collective self-confidence in feeling good about what you are doing. It means people are getting better services and, in the end, that is what is most important.

Q: *Looking back, what would you have done differently?*

A: In certain Common Ground Sanctuary programs, I wish I would have done evaluation earlier as opposed to later in the programs' histories. Now we are doing evaluation with programs even if we are not required to do it.

Central Massachusetts Oral Health Initiative

▶ Improve Service Quality

Influence Policy and Legislation

Market a Program

Program

Central Massachusetts Oral Health Initiative (CMOHI), a coalition of organizations organized by the University of Massachusetts Medical School in Worcester, Massachusetts, has two main goals: 1) to increase access to oral health services for individuals on Medicaid or who are uninsured and 2) to serve as a role model for oral health services that can be replicated across the state and thus increase access for oral health services statewide.

To meet these goals, the coalition provides direct oral health services through a volunteer program and school-based preventive programs, and advocates for legislative change to address oral health policy issues at the state level.

Evaluation

The coalition conducts an annual evaluation in addition to monthly and bimonthly reporting on ongoing programmatic outcomes. Since its inception, CMOHI has been collecting certain demographic information along with utilization data. The program conducts evaluations of its services at the request of its major funder.

Evaluation use—Improve service quality

CMOHI's steering committee meets approximately once every other month to examine program outcomes and determine what program improvements would strengthen the Initiative's services. For example, after the committee and the evaluator looked at participation numbers in a school district for one of its oral health programs, the evaluator examined the process for returning permissions slips. After recognizing that many children and their teachers were not following through, program staff added an incentive for both children and teachers to increase the return of permission slips, which then increased program participation.

Another example involved the method of providing fluoride treatment to children. Originally, one of the agencies offered fluoride rinses weekly in the schools. Other schools would not undertake this method of delivery because it required too much time away from classroom learning. After researching alternatives, CMOHI experimented with fluoride varnishes, an application that is fast, yet needs to be done only two or three times per year. With this switch, the evaluator has shown that the Initiative can treat more children than it would have done under the initial application method.

Questions and answers

Q: *What barriers did you experience in using evaluation results, and how did you overcome these barriers?*

A: We experienced barriers to collecting data for the evaluation. A lot of agencies we worked with were not used to collecting the type of data we needed to examine our outcomes. In particular, data collection for negative consequences (when a permission slip is not returned) is not generally collected. The agencies could report frequency of permissions given and services provided on returned permission slips, but that was only part of the picture. Part of this issue was addressed by the fact that we pay agencies additional funds to provide data, as stated in our contracts with them. After agencies found out the data collection was more time consuming than expected, the Initiative increased the amount of money they provided for evaluation purposes. This made a difference by increasing the staff and resources necessary for appropriate evaluation data collection. Since it is part of the contractual agreement, agencies knew they needed to provide it.

Q: *What advice do you have for programs that hope to use their evaluation results in similar ways?*

A: There are two things that have been useful to us. One, set up some goals up front—something to measure your work against. With the schools program, we targeted how many kids we thought we could treat. Then we compared our target with actual numbers. Also, use the data and look at it. Do not wait for a year to look at your data. It is important to continually check data and compare it with goals and outcomes to see how you are doing. In our program, the data was also useful for examining the sustainability of our initiatives. Since we are grant-funded and know these funds will eventually no longer be available, the data helped us predict whether we would be able to continue certain initiatives.

Q: *What is the most important thing you have learned through your evaluation activities?*

A: You can make changes midway through your program. When you have evaluation results staring you in the face and saying you need to make a change, do it.

Q: *Looking back, what would you have done differently?*

A: We might have better refined our goals. We learned that it is important to make goals more attainable. Don't make them too much of a stretch. Also, we meet every other month now. It used to be that we met monthly, which was not as helpful. We have learned to focus on different program elements in different meetings. This has helped us to discuss just a few places where we could make improvements rather than to keep looking at the overall program at every meeting.

Q: *Anything else?*

A: It does not hurt to have your evaluator at the table. Many times we did not include the evaluator at the beginning, but later realized that evaluators point out things that others might not notice. Now we view the evaluator as part of our team. Some staff might have viewed the evaluator as someone who is checking over their shoulders to make sure they are doing the right things. We learned not to see it like that. We found it useful that the evaluator provided a different perspective on how to improve the program.

Targeted Early Intervention	▶ Improve Service Quality
	Influence Policy and Legislation
	Market a Program

Program

Targeted Early Intervention—an initiative located in the Twin Cities, Minnesota, including the Hennepin County Attorney's Office; Children, Family, and Adult Services; Economic Assistance; and Community Health—works to prevent future delinquency among Hennepin County youth. To meet this goal, staff and contracted providers offer intensive, long-term services to families of county residents under the age of ten who have committed crimes and are at high risk for future delinquency. While initially designed as a pilot project, in 2004 the Targeted Early Intervention initiative was integrated into the day-to-day operations of the Human Services and Public Health Department (a newly formed department, which included the former departments of Children, Family, and Adult Services; Economic Assistance; and Community Health).

Evaluation

Since the program began in April 1997, two evaluations have been conducted. The first evaluation focused on program implementation; the second evaluation focused on outcomes for youth in the program, more specifically whether or not the program was meeting its desired outcomes. One of the main reasons the second evaluation was conducted is because the program was a new approach, and it was important to let the public know whether it worked or not.

Evaluation use—Improve service quality

Targeted Early Intervention used the second evaluation to improve the program by examining what had been implemented after the first evaluation and determining whether or not the changes made were successful. The evaluation also enabled the program to decide what should be implemented in the future.

Questions and answers

Q: *What barriers did you experience in using evaluation results, and how did you overcome these barriers?*

A: One of the biggest barriers was the struggle I had in reconciling the evaluation of the program as implemented versus the evaluation of the program as designed. We did many things differently than we had initially anticipated. When it came to evaluating, we reported initially that we thought this particular design was going to work. Later, we reported that the program was working, but not the way it was originally designed. People would contact us, say the original design was a good idea, and ask if we were doing it. It became a hybrid evaluation, telling us how much of the original design we had implemented and, since we didn't, how well what we were doing was working.

Another barrier is that service providers are pretty resistant to change, even if change may improve things in the long run. Even if the evaluation says you really need to have a mental health person doing assessments on all of these kids, what we hear is the mental health person working on the team saying, "That's not what I was told I would do when I came on, and that's not my role." It was a real struggle, and I can honestly say that it has not been resolved. It's still as big an obstacle as it initially was.

Because of the nature of the project, there were always questions about whether it was worth the investment and rumors that the program might fold. This created anxiety among the staff, so they focused on justifying their existence instead of the needs of the families. That had an effect on the evaluation, but it's impossible to quantify. Staff were stressed out about wanting the evaluation to be positive because if it wasn't, they wouldn't be around. Their ownership of the outcomes was much greater because they had this constant feeling of being threatened.

Q: *What advice do you have for programs that hope to use their evaluation results in similar ways?*

A: Programs need to be aware of the financial implications for implementing the results. One of the things that we saw was that, while we were investing a ton of resources in these kids, we probably should be investing more. How do we do that when it's already one of the richest programs in the county? I'm not sure how you anticipate that; it is a no-brainer that you could always use more money. Getting the evaluation that says you have to invest more resources is hard, because one of the questions from the policymakers is what are you doing with the money now?

Q: *What is the most important thing you have learned through your evaluation activities?*

A: Be clear about whether or not you need to evaluate the program as it was designed or as it was implemented; know the implications of that choice.

Q: *Looking back, what would you have done differently?*

A: One of the things that I allowed to happen was that the evaluation results were too influenced by the staff working on the project, by their self-imposed boundaries and roles. As a result, we evaluated more along what they did because that's how they wanted it done. I would have played hardball a little bit more and said that what people want to know is whether the project as we designed it is working, and we need to stick a little more closely to evaluating (and implementing) the design.

For Your Consideration:
Using Results to Improve Service Quality

If you want to use program evaluation to improve the quality of services you provide, you may want to consider the following questions.

At a minimum, can you demonstrate the following:

- The number of people you serve?
- Their major social/demographic characteristics?
- The problems/needs your clients have that you can address?
- The amount and types of services your clients receive from you?
- The percentage of clients for whom you met the need, or resolved the problem, that they brought to you?
- Does your evaluation monitor outcomes consistently over time?

Does your evaluation provide the type of information that will enable you to know

- Your overall effectiveness?
- Your effectiveness with specific groups (for example, men or women, different racial or ethnic groups, and so on)?
- Do you apply, in your planning, the evaluation results obtained by similar programs?
- Do you look for evidence-based practices (service delivery methods whose effectiveness is well documented) and use them if they exist? (This is a way to incorporate the evaluation research of others into your work.)
- How do you make the use of evaluation findings part of a process within your organization to continuously improve your services?
- Do you have staff meetings and discussion focused on the evaluation findings and what they mean?
- Do you encourage decision making based on the data?
- Have you developed ways that staff, as individuals, can use the data in their work with clients?
- Do you constantly explore the need for special approaches for specific groups (Southeast Asians, suburban residents, and so forth)?

Using Evaluation Results to Influence Policy and Legislation

Evaluation findings, such as program outcomes, can be communicated to policymakers to influence policy and legislative decisions. Evaluation data can demonstrate to public officials and their aides which programs can, and cannot, effectively meet needs or have an impact on a community. Evaluation data presented to the general public can influence the constituents of public officials—who will then let their officials know the facts. Evaluation data presented to funders can influence their overall funding policies and priorities.

As one program staff member explained to us, "We have been able to use evaluation and research to change public policy and legislation. Before the time of evaluation, mayors and other public officials always heard anecdotal information about a program. And while that information may be truthful, grouped data—more concrete information—describes what the vast majority are experiencing. Because we can demonstrate numbers and data, we are able to influence policy and legislation."

Influencing policy and legislation offers you the opportunity to make a difference in the overall funding of services, enabling the community in which you work to better meet the needs of its population. Such influence can affect the system of allocating resources specifically to your organization. In addition, by educating public officials and other decision makers about the evaluation results, you raise their awareness of the needs of the people you serve. They may become more sympathetic concerning those needs—not just with respect to the services you provide, but overall.

The organizations that follow have made excellent use of their evaluative information to shape and influence the regulations and legislation that impact their mission.

Rural Opportunities, Inc.—Pennsylvania

Improve Service Quality
▶ Influence Policy and Legislation
Market a Program

Program

Rural Opportunities, Inc. is a national organization with several state offices including the state office in Pennsylvania interviewed for this book. Rural Opportunities has several employment programs, including the National Farmworkers Jobs Program (NFJP). This program, which began in 1978, provides job training opportunities and customized skill training to help migrant and seasonal adult farmworkers find employment outside of agriculture.

Evaluation

NFJP does both "internal" and "external" evaluation. A program staff person does ongoing monitoring for regular quality control. An external evaluator conducts an annual review, measuring specific achievements. NFJP has four major purposes for doing evaluation: 1) to make sure it meets funding requirements, 2) to ensure that the program is cost-effective, 3) to maintain operations that fit within the mission statement, and 4) to make sure that the program optimizes the direct services provided to participants.

Evaluation use—Influence policy and legislation

NFJP uses evaluation results to educate legislators about how taxpayer dollars are paying for a successful program. Evaluation results enable program staff to show that the program is performing well, not just based on verbal statements, but also on internal and external evaluation data. By showing the success of the program, staff hope to influence policymakers to consider replicating the employment model in other areas in need of similar services.

Related to this, each time the NFJP has a new program it is interested in developing and funding, its board of directors reviews the potential program's goals to ensure that they are consistent with the overall mission of the organization. The board also reviews potential programs for their cost-effectiveness. These steps ensure that decisions concerning NFJP funding are thoughtful and deliberate. They strengthen the credibility of the organization in the eyes of public officials and the general public.

Questions and answers

Q: *What barriers have you experienced in using evaluation results, and how did you overcome those barriers?*

A: The main barrier we have is collecting a massive amount of information and designing a process based on our evaluation materials to be user-friendly and comprehensive. We have found that some of our tools worked against us because they were not user-friendly; they were too open to interpretation. When we first began this project, it was a barrier to create an effective tool, whereas now we constantly revise our evaluation tools. For other programs with similar issues, I would suggest starting off with a basic, user-friendly evaluation tool that asks specific questions, nothing open-ended or too general.

Q: *What advice do you have for programs hoping to use their evaluation results in similar ways?*

A: No matter what level of management you are, you will appreciate being able to review the effectiveness of the total program and to see that all systems are being held accountable. No matter how far along the program is, make sure you have an evaluation tool created. Also, it is better to have someone that is not directly in the program be involved with the evaluation process.

Q: *What is the most important thing you have learned through your evaluation activities?*

A: It may be common sense to some, but not until you have put yourself through the whole process will you completely understand the evaluation process. It makes you realize that every management level is accountable to some degree. It is also helpful for many staff to review the effectiveness of our quality and our programming.

Q: *Looking back, what would you have done differently?*

A: I wish we had more flexibility to make changes to the tools. Another thing, our mission statement was too general, so not only did the tool need to be tweaked, our mission needed to be tweaked.

Q: Anything else?

A: As part of a multi-state national organization, we began evaluating programs in a formal way about ten years ago. Not only did we evaluate our programs, we also looked at the life cycle of the project. It has been difficult to find an evaluation tool already out there that would work for programs or organizations such as ours. For-profit businesses examine specific products. There is no similar monitoring tool for nonprofits.

McKnight Foundation's Welfare to Work Initiative	
	Improve Service Quality
	▶ Influence Policy and Legislation
	Market a Program

Program

The McKnight Foundation launched its Welfare to Work Initiative in January 1998, funding twenty-two support networks for individuals transitioning from welfare to work. These networks operate in eighty-six counties throughout Minnesota and are composed of social service providers, employers, technical and community colleges, job trainers, religious organizations, government agencies, and others who facilitate movement into the workforce. Network members coordinate their activities to provide a variety of services to individuals making the transition. These services include job training, job mentoring, personal mentoring, transportation assistance, and help finding child care. In addition, the networks offer assistance to employers working to accommodate their new employees. The major goal of the Welfare to Work Initiative, according to a senior program officer at the McKnight Foundation, is to help people moving from welfare to work "find jobs and keep them," and to "otherwise improve their lives." The Foundation hoped to involve not only the people it was trying to help with the initiative, but also a larger segment of the community, which is why it required representation from different sectors. Over time, the Foundation found that the community as a whole became more understanding of individuals on welfare.

Evaluation

The McKnight Foundation contracted with an external evaluator to assess the impact of the Welfare to Work Initiative in its first three years. Staff at the foundation wanted to know which parts of the initiative were working, which parts were not working, and why. This information would help them decide what kinds of programs to support in the future. In addition, foundation staff wanted to ensure that they would have evidence to bring to policymakers should the initiative be successful. A final motivation for evaluating the Welfare to Work Initiative was the McKnight Foundation's desire to help other organizations in Minnesota to improve their services and supports for people moving from welfare to work.

The evaluation tracked the experiences of participants, both the services they received and the success they had in finding stable employment.

Evaluation use—Influence policy and legislation

With regard to influencing policy, the Welfare to Work evaluation was useful on several levels. Even before the final results were available, some networks used information from the evaluation to promote improvements in their counties' administrative regulations. For instance, one network persuaded a county to make child care payments in a timelier manner, when they were needed by parents. At the state level, the McKnight Foundation presented decision makers with findings from an interim evaluation report, including evidence that support services should be tailored to the needs of individuals entering the workforce. The foundation pointed out that the kind of personalized assistance provided by their networks entailed flexible funding and "different kinds of solutions in different areas." As a result, the state allocated what was termed "welfare transition money" to counties throughout Minnesota to support activities similar to those of the McKnight networks.

Questions and answers

Q: *What advice do you have for programs hoping to use their evaluation results in similar ways?*

A: Evaluation is key for programs that hope to affect policy decisions. Policymakers want some evidence that things work. In addition, the evidence must be credible—the product of sound research studies. Human service programs are often limited in the kinds of study designs they can employ. But it can be effective to measure the same outcome in more than one way. If you measure two or three different ways and come up with similar results, it's much stronger.

In conducting evaluations, a very close and frequent relationship should exist between program staff and the research team. Such a relationship ensures that the two groups are in agreement on what's being evaluated and how it's being done. A strong relationship is also helpful when researchers and program staff must deal with unexpected challenges. There are always some surprises in the evaluation process. While working on the Welfare to Work evaluation, staff at the McKnight Foundation grew concerned that the research team was taking too much time from the network members participating in the study. Because McKnight Foundation staff were in close contact with the research team, they were able to voice this concern and work with the researchers to find a solution.

The McKnight Foundation has also found an advisory committee to be helpful in planning evaluation studies. Committee members provide different perspectives and expertise to the research team. Deciding who should be on the committee depends on the topic and what you hope to accomplish. You want some people there who have firsthand knowledge of whatever it is that you're studying—front-line workers or managers. It's also helpful, when possible, to have the ultimate service users or recipients involved—whoever you're hoping to benefit. Because we hope to affect policy with our evaluation results, we also like to have people who are involved in policy on the committee. We want them to know what's happening, and we want to learn from them how to do this in a way that will appeal to policy people. In addition, advisory committees assembled by the McKnight Foundation usually include a McKnight staff person and at least one academic with expertise in the area of interest.

SMILES

Improve Service Quality
▶ Influence Policy and Legislation
Market a Program

Program

Since its inception in 1994, SMILES, a program of Dental Health for Arlington, Inc. located in Arlington, Texas, has worked to improve the oral health of low-income children. The SMILES program provides screening in schools and applies sealants to students in school. Children receiving SMILES services attend schools that have at least 50 percent of their students on the free lunch program, which currently includes 24 schools. In 2003, more than 5,800 children in first, second, and third grades received these services.

Evaluation

Recently, SMILES participated in evaluations with the Pew Partnership for Civic Change and the Texas Department of Health. SMILES wanted to make sure its program was improving the oral health of the children it served. The evaluation examined the extent to which SMILES reduced the incidence of decay. While the program understood that low-income children often do not receive dental care, they wanted to know the reasons children were not going to the dentist. In a blind study, teachers were asked to judge both the academic performance and classroom behavior of students with severe decay compared to those in need of only routine care.

Evaluation use—Influence policy and legislation

Dental Health for Arlington works with Tarrant County on the Children's Oral Health Coalition, which advocates for improved dental coverage for low-income children in Texas. This coalition uses a "white paper" essay to educate legislators about specific issues. Evaluation results are included in each essay to help demonstrate the need for increased dental care coverage for low-income children and to show the effectiveness of the specific program.

Through its program evaluation, the organization has been able to demonstrate that it does reduce tooth decay rates. Evaluation has also shown prevention produces significantly better outcomes at lower costs. These findings are highlighted in the organization's presentations that advocate for new policies and legislation.

Questions and answers

Q: *What barriers have you experienced in using evaluation results, and how did you overcome those barriers?*

A: The only barrier that we encountered came from the parameters stated in one contract. The entity paying for the research was prepared to let the university researchers use only the final statistics that were generated from the project. The researchers wanted to be able to use the research, which they created, in their professional papers as well. We worked with lawyers from both sides to create an alternative plan that enabled us to continue working with the university in a way that satisfied the requirements of both entities.

Q: *What advice do you have for programs hoping to use their evaluation results in similar ways?*

A: Choose your researcher very carefully. Make sure you understand each other well. Agree on who will be in charge and write down your shared understandings before starting the evaluation work. Also, do not try to reinvent the wheel. One reason our research projects were feasible and practical for our staff was because the researcher made data gathering easy. She found ways to roll the evaluation into what we were already doing.

Q: *What is the most important thing you have learned through your evaluation activities?*

A: I'm the person who is responsible for funding. Funders, the community, and board members know you're on top of things if you're constantly evaluating your programs. Evaluation shows that you are not just sliding along, doing the same thing you have always done. Evaluation shows your partners that you are trying to learn about your performance and how to improve outcomes as much as possible. If you are doing authentic research with a credible partner, then everyone recognizes that reliable evaluation results carry weight when an organization claims its programs are working. These strategies make a big difference in your ability to fund your programs.

Q: *Looking back, what would you have done differently?*

A: Pew Partnership was kind enough to provide us with training on how to market our evaluation. If you do an evaluation and keep it on the shelf, it means nothing. They helped us make our program's work more visible. I still only know a small part about marketing. Looking back, I would have liked to know more about marketing evaluation results, so that I could have started planning that piece much earlier in the process.

Q: *Anything else?*

A: When you have never done an evaluation, it seems like a big mystery in the beginning. It's not rocket science, but it is hard to know what to do. If you have the luxury of the services of a trained evaluator, then it is not difficult. It can make a big difference in your program in terms of getting funding and other support. You can prove that your program works.

Housing First	Improve Service Quality
	▶ Influence Policy and Legislation
	Market a Program

Program

Housing First, a program of Beyond Shelter located in Los Angeles, California, began in 1988 as a new approach to address homelessness at both the family level and the systemic level. Housing First helps homeless families move into permanent and affordable housing as quickly as possible and provides intensive, time-limited support services to help with stabilization. In addition to providing social services, Housing First has established itself as a laboratory for system change, with staff implementing new approaches or reintroducing old approaches to address individual and systemic issues of homelessness.

Evaluation

Since the Housing First program began, Beyond Shelter has conducted evaluation to test the program's methodology and to give credibility to its service approaches. Over time, staff monitor families as they go through the program. The evaluation identifies whether each family's situation improves and the specific ways in which families benefit from the program. A key measure involves whether clients achieve housing stability and sustain it.

Evaluation use—Influence policy and legislation

Evaluation is instrumental for validating the approaches that are used to implement the Housing First program. The tracking and evaluation of these approaches enable Housing First staff to inform public policy and organizational practices.

Due in part to credible evaluation findings for Housing First, the president and CEO of Beyond Shelter has worked closely with a number of national advocacy groups focused on addressing homelessness. Most notably, she serves on the advisory committee of the National Alliance to End Homelessness, an advocacy group that influences policy decisions in Washington, DC.

Based on its initial work and results during demonstration project phases, Housing First made a positive impression on the U.S. Department of Housing and Urban Development (HUD). In addition to educating HUD about new approaches for addressing family homelessness, Housing First has provided education on the topic to other government agencies that serve low-income families, including the U.S. Department of Health and Human Services and the U.S. Department of Labor.

Through evaluation, Housing First provides a model that can be adapted by other organizations. This is a "policy" influence in the sense that it changes the ways that organizations serving the homeless do their work. As noted by the president and CEO, "I do not believe in best practices or replication, but I do believe in adaptation. You can adopt a new system by using the adaptable components that have been demonstrated to work and applying them to a new program. The reason you do not want replication but adaptation is because, in a given geographic area, funding and political changes can occur. Unless you have an adaptable mechanism to respond to those changes, your organization will not experience the same outcomes supported by previous evaluation results. Also, a program must be adaptable and flexible to change as new ways of doing things develop. If a program is not adaptable, how will it promote change or impact policy?"

In 1996, HUD chose Beyond Shelter's Housing First Program as one of the "25 U.S. Best Practices" for the United Nations Conference, *Habitat II*, held in Istanbul, Turkey. The program was chosen specifically for its effectiveness demonstrated by credible evaluation.

Questions and answers

Q: *What advice do you have for programs hoping to use their evaluation results in similar ways?*

A: Design your evaluation with researchers who understand evaluation, and make sure you provide a lot of input in the design process. Understand how to track information, enter it, and process it so it is usable for you. Research needs a combination of narrative information and data. Sometimes the most important part of a report is the narrative interpretation of the data. Data may be great by itself, but it may be stronger when provided within the context of why the program exists and who it is serving. Sometimes academic partners may not be able to write a compelling report showing this link. It's okay to do such work in-house, if you have the staff.

Q: *What is the most important thing you have learned through your evaluation activities?*

A: Evaluation results give your program credibility and help initiate new development. Because we continue to apply new ideas for addressing homelessness, evaluation is necessary and important to convince others to accept the efficacy of new approaches. Early in the development of Housing First, I implemented a series of projects to evaluate the Housing First methodology. Some of the employment projects ended in failure, but when I figured out which methods were successful, I received a sizable grant from the Department of Labor to implement the program on a national level, evaluate the success of such approaches, and disseminate the findings.

Q: *Anything else?*

A: We focused on certain intentions and then discovered other uses for evaluation results, such as educating funders, proving a point, or being able to emphasize system change more than expected. With the evaluation, we identified areas that we did not initially realize were important but then saw the need to evaluate further. For example, we have a high success rate with a particular population with many unmet needs. As a result, we are trying to create another evaluation over a two- or three-year period to track their progress and needs more closely.

PACE Center for Girls	
	Improve Service Quality
	▶ Influence Policy and Legislation
	Market a Program

Program

Since 1985, PACE (Practical Academic Cultural Education) Center for Girls, located in Jacksonville, Florida, assists girls and adolescent women between the ages of eight and eighteen to remain free of negative behaviors such as violence and crime, and to pursue education and increase employability. Services provided by the program include values and ethics education, counseling, parental partnerships, and case management services. PACE experienced a period of tremendous growth during the 1990s, going from three storefronts with a $900,000 annual budget to a $20 million operation with requests from state government to open more centers. Since its inception, the program has been replicated almost twenty times across the state of Florida.

Evaluation

PACE is evaluated annually, both through internal evaluation activities and through external evaluations done by the Department of Juvenile Justice. Early in its expansion stage, the program sought an outside evaluator to assist them in assessing the strengths and areas of need for the agency.

PACE developed "Standards of Excellence," specific benchmarks derived by data collection and evaluation, in seven domains. PACE collects data to measure progress in these seven domains, which influence strategic planning and management decisions. The Department of Juvenile Justice's annual evaluation shows that PACE routinely meets or exceeds its outcomes, and, as a result, it is rated a great program in Florida for young girls.

Evaluation use—Influence policy and legislation

In 2004, PACE was successful in helping pass a bill in the state of Florida that mandates state provision of such services for girls. This bill passed due, in part, to the outcomes from PACE's evaluation. PACE introduced the legislation, did the advocacy work, and used their research and evaluation data to move this policy forward.

PACE uses evaluation outcomes to inform people that they are supporting a program that works. In their public speaking and conferences across the country, staff present evaluation results to show that the program is successful. To influence practice in the field, PACE Center also provides training and technical assistance services to organizations across the country.

Questions and answers

Q: *What barriers have you experienced in using evaluation results, and how did you overcome those barriers?*

A: One of the major barriers was getting staff buy-in for the evaluation. It just seemed like another added thing on their workload. We mitigated this by taking the time to do several staff retreats where they had input about the evaluation process.

Technology capacity has been another barrier for us in using evaluation results the way we would like. As part of our strategic direction, we are trying to expand our technology capacity, but we have issues around funding and staff training for technology. Right now we have a program where we collect all our data from the nineteen centers throughout the state of Florida. We would like to move to a web-based system where we can access all information through the state office. This would allow us to look at trends and see if our local centers are meeting the established benchmarks for the Standards of Excellence. Several things right now are housed in different places, and an integrated technology system would help improve our evaluation analysis and reporting immensely.

Q: *What advice do you have for programs hoping to use their evaluation results in similar ways?*

A: First, engage key stakeholders in the planning process so they buy-in and understand the connection between data collection, evaluation, and program outcomes of the direct services provided by the program.

Q: *What is the most important thing you have learned through your evaluation activities?*

A: By using evaluation results, we stay focused on what matters most. We are able to strategically move forward because evaluation focuses us as opposed to making decisions based on people's opinions or perceptions. We can look at the trend lines in the data as concrete information that keeps us focused on our work.

Q: *Looking back, what would you have done differently?*

A: I wish I would have started evaluation sooner, when we were a smaller organization. Then, as the organization had grown, we would have already established evaluation as a part of our work culture. By implementing evaluation during the middle of our growing period, it was harder to integrate it into our culture.

Q: *Anything else?*

A: When we originally started the evaluation, I saw its use in a very limited way. I understood that we would be able to use it for recording and paperwork. I did not envision it to be the expansive way we use it now with our Standards of Excellence and our benchmarks.

**For Your Consideration:
Using Results to Influence Policy and Legislation**

*If you want to use program evaluation to influence policy and legislation,
you may want to consider the following:*

- Does the design and revision of your evaluation process include involvement of all stakeholders who might want to use the data?

- Have you involved policymakers and/or their staff on evaluation advisory committees?

- Do you understand the questions that public officials want answered regarding service effectiveness, and do you know what they consider good evidence?

- Do you routinely consult evaluation findings from other organizations and combine the findings with your own to produce a stronger result?

- Do you and your staff have confidence in your ability to provide expert testimony based on evaluation findings, if necessary?

- Do you publish data in an easy-to-use format, such as a newsletter, that decision makers can quickly consult and understand?

- Do you formulate your evaluation and present the results in the vocabulary of policymakers?

- What have you done to ensure that your evaluation is seen as completely nonpartisan?

- Is your method similar enough to other evaluation research so that you can combine findings and strengthen their impact on legislators?

- Do you include cost information along with your outcome information to give a picture of cost-effectiveness?

Using Evaluation Results to Market a Program

Some organizations have used the results of evaluation studies to market their programs' services, and ultimately, to increase their revenues. This means communicating to potential clients or consumers about the results of an organization's services, in order to influence more of them to use those services.

One way they have done this is to communicate evaluation findings on outcomes of a program or a service to grantmakers or to purchasers in order to generate more (or larger) grants or more purchases.

Sometimes, solely for accountability, minimal evaluation results must be reported to funding agencies. Other times, you may be in competition with other organizations. Strong, credible evaluation results can provide a competitive edge in either of these cases.

The organizations that follow made good use of evaluation to promote their programs. Mounds View Even Start was able to halt a funder's cancellation of grants by sharing its program effectiveness data. Street-Wise Partners uses its evaluation results to maintain current donors and attract new ones, to influence internal stakeholders, and to demonstrate its flexibility. Shreveport-Bossier Community Renewal includes evaluation information in multiple promotional vehicles including annual reports, presentations, and site tours. Woodland Hills uses its evaluation results to retain and gain new business.

Mounds View Even Start

Improve Service Quality
Influence Policy and Legislation
▶ Market a Program

Program

Mounds View Even Start, which began in the early 1990s, aims to help low-income parents achieve one or more of the following goals: break the cycle of intergenerational illiteracy; get high school credentials, either through a GED or diploma; realize they are their children's first teacher; help them become better parents; and help their children be ready for school success. Mounds View Even Start provides services such as early childhood education, parenting classes, activities that foster parent and child together time, adult-based education, and transportation to and from classes to help parents and their children achieve these goals.

Evaluation

The Mounds View Even Start program is evaluated by a professional third-party evaluator, as mandated by the federal government.

Evaluation use—Market a program

By showing that the program was successful through evaluation results, Mounds View Even Start was able to strengthen its funding opportunities with both current and prospective funders. According to the program manager, in 2004 key funders had considered discontinuing funding for Even Start, due to limited resources. In response, Mounds View Even Start shared its program evaluation results with the funders. The numbers demonstrated how successful and necessary the program's services were to families. Funders were influenced by these findings, and as a result, the program continued to receive financial support. (Note: Since third quarter 2006, this program's funding situation has changed. The program is currently operating at reduced capacity. In 2004, however, Mounds View Even Start's ability to demonstrate its program's success through evaluation findings was impactive in preventing program cuts.)

Questions and answers

Q: *What advice do you have for programs hoping to use their evaluation results in similar ways?*

A: Develop the evaluation to make it work for the program, not to make it look good for somebody else. Make sure the evaluation helps you learn what you want to know and gather the type of results that will be most helpful for your organization.

Q: *What is the most important thing you have learned through your evaluation activities?*

A: An evaluation is a snapshot of the program. It is a photograph of how consumers see the service as beneficial to them. Their perception might be different from ours, but it is their perception of the value of our services. We need to know that point of view.

Q: *Looking back, what would you have done differently?*

A: I could have done things to make the evaluation process easier. Having a chart or checklist would help me make sure we are on time and on target with whatever we need to be evaluating at different points in the year. I need to do a better job of making the process more efficient and complete in accessing data.

Q: *Anything else?*

A: When I first started, I saw evaluation as a requirement of our grant. I did not see it as a tool that could benefit us. Within the first year of learning how comprehensive and well done the evaluation was, I saw it as a useful tool in helping us understand how to modify our program. It is not just a requirement; it is a good tool.

Evaluation has been a useful and authentic tool for us to learn how we can improve our program. Working with a research center that understands sociological problems helped us to create an evaluation tool that was appropriate for us. The evaluator we work with understands that it is people first, numbers second, but that numbers help explain people's stories.

StreetWise Partners

Improve Service Quality
Influence Policy and Legislation
▶ Market a Program

Program

StreetWise Partners, located in New York City, provides mentoring opportunities and job skills training to disadvantaged adults who need help finding and maintaining employment. The organization, which began in 1997, provides computer training, career development services, intensive mentoring and job coaching, and ongoing support services until people are employed. StreetWise Partners targets adults eighteen or older who are low-income or otherwise disadvantaged.

Evaluation

StreetWise Partners conducts an ongoing evaluation. The evaluation includes a mail or phone survey to learn about the employment situation of program graduates. The organization tracks two things: 1) the students' knowledge and skills during and after the program, and 2) the graduates' ability to obtain jobs and advance in jobs. StreetWise Partners evaluates its services to maintain contact with graduates and to ensure that the program adequately prepares people for employment.

Evaluation use—Market a program

StreetWise Partners receives a large amount of its funding from individual donors. These donors want to know how the organization is using its dollars to successfully serve adults with employment needs. As a result, funders want statistics that show the program's success; evaluation statistics meet this demand. By including evaluation results in its marketing to current and future donors, the program strengthens its visibility as a successful organization and increases its revenue.

In addition, StreetWise Partners uses evaluation results to demonstrate to funders its ability to change to meet the needs of its clientele. For example, after learning from employed graduates about the need for a monthly support group to help individuals recently placed in jobs, StreetWise Partners created such a group. Ongoing evaluation helps the organization determine the areas in which students and graduates need assistance, whether job searching, skill development, or other areas related to employment. The program then adds services to address these needs.

"Marketing" also occurs within the organization when the executive director keeps volunteers and board members informed about evaluation results. This has become increasingly important as the organization has grown and undergone change. When the program first began, board members had regular contact with program students and graduates. Now, due to organizational changes, the board works separately from the program clients but wishes to maintain a strong connection with clients and graduates. Evaluation results help board members understand how graduates are doing. Results also help board members feel satisfied with the program's work, which motivates them to continue providing time and energy to the board.

Questions and answers

Q: *What is the most important thing you have learned through your evaluation activities?*

A: The biggest lesson we have learned is asking the right questions. While it's necessary to use black-and-white language, it is easy to ask questions that are too simplistic. When we are working with the students in our program, it is important to talk with them about the services they are receiving. We also ask ourselves what we want to get out of the data and what we want to use it for.

Q: *Looking back, what would you have done differently?*

A: We do the evaluation in-house, getting clients and volunteers to help. We have not in the past nor do we now organize the results as much as I would like. It would be nice to hire someone for a year to help gather evaluation results. This would help me to appreciate the consistency of getting an evaluation report.

Q: *Anything else?*

A: We designed our evaluation system using the Kellogg Foundation's logic model. It's a great logic model that funders recognize. If you get to the point where you have output, outcomes, indicators, and impact that you're measuring, then you should be able to measure the benefits of the program yourself.

Shreveport-Bossier Community Renewal

Improve Service Quality

Influence Policy and Legislation

▶ Market a Program

Program

Shreveport-Bossier Community Renewal, located in Shreveport and Bossier, Louisiana, has the mission to restore the foundation of a safe and caring community by rebuilding the neighborhood system of caring relationships. A comprehensive community initiative that began in 1994, the organization has three strategies for meeting its mission. One strategy, the Internal Care Unit Strategy, focuses on rebuilding capacity in geographic neighborhoods by sending full-time staff to live in the neighborhood.

Evaluation

Since 2002, Shreveport-Bossier Community Renewal has been collecting evaluation data to measure whether it meets specific objectives it has for the communities it serves. Evaluation identifies the characteristics of the neighborhoods' populations (the number of adults and children, the number of unemployed, and so on) to determine what changes are occurring in neighborhoods and how the organization's programs and services should change in response. Then, the data indicate whether improvements seem to be occurring.

The evaluation gathers data in addition to census information. For example, since one of the main outcomes Shreveport-Bossier Community Renewal wanted to achieve was to develop a system of caring relationships, they have measured the frequency and duration of relationships developing in a community. Shreveport-Bossier tracks children's accomplishments and leadership abilities. They track children's capacity to take on leadership roles within their peer groups in order to determine whether that capacity increases over time.

Evaluation use—Market a program

Like most nonprofits, Shreveport-Bossier has a number of stakeholders including its board, the general public, and donors. All these stakeholders are interested in knowing the results of evaluation, so the organization provides information to them so they can be informed and encouraged about the program's work. In addition to producing a yearly report, the program staff also develops PowerPoint presentations, binders with information, handouts, and tours using evaluation data to make sure that evaluation information is readily available to stakeholders.

Questions and answers

Q: *What barriers have you experienced in using evaluation results, and how did you overcome those barriers?*

A: Sometimes the timing was an issue for us—being able to get the right information to the right people at the right time. It has always been a challenge in an organization that has many people involved. We try to provide reports as soon as possible.

Another problem is using census data for our work. Census data is outdated as soon as you get it, especially for neighborhoods that are transitional. We have a smaller area than a census tract might include, and trying to extrapolate about a smaller area with X income, when that area does not fit a census tract, is difficult.

A third barrier we've noticed is that communicating evaluation information to staff members, especially about performance, can cause frustration when evaluation reflects the program poorly. We get staff to look at this as a way to improve the communities; we try to get the results to them on time, so they can use them.

Q: *What advice do you have for programs hoping to use their evaluation results in similar ways?*

A: Develop communication with staff members. Explain the purpose of data collection and involve them as much as possible. Make sure people do not get results late. If that happens, the results may not be very helpful.

Q: *What is the most important thing you have learned through your evaluation activities?*

A: It is a necessary part of any organization, and time must be set aside to do it. It has to be given that priority right from the top.

Q: *Anything else?*

A: When you are starting out in a new direction, think about the kinds of data you would need to collect from the beginning. Consider the method, the type of data collection, and when to advance or change the evaluation based on not needing to collect certain data anymore. Sometimes you have to be reminded that data does not need to be collected anymore. Periodically ask yourself if the data is still relevant.

Woodland Hills	Improve Service Quality
	Influence Policy and Legislation
	▶ Market a Program

Program

Founded in 1909, Woodland Hills, located in Duluth, Minnesota, offers a continuum of care for adolescents in a strength-based, peer-empowerment environment. The organization's mission is to reduce risk factors, cultivate assets, and build on the strengths of all youth and their families to help them lead successful lives. Specific services provided by the per diem programs include day treatment, residential treatment, and transitional services that help young people, males and females ages twelve to twenty, learn new value systems and skills to make appropriate choices. Woodland Hills also operates a free, voluntary program called Neighborhood Youth Services that engages diverse youth by offering hope, a sense of belonging, and opportunities to help youth reach their full potential.

Evaluation

Woodland Hills tracks measures internally and relies on county data for recidivism information. Woodland Hills opted to develop a regular evaluation of its services because its customers were looking for cost-effective placement options with good results. While the agency knew it was providing quality services, it lacked a means of reporting those services. Through the assistance of an outside evaluator, the program developed evaluation measures that looked specifically at progress youth make while they are in Woodland Hills programs.

Evaluation use—Market a program

With regard to marketing strategies, as budgets tightened due to cuts at the legislative level, the agency recognized the need to market its outcomes to retain and gain new business.

One of Woodland Hills' goals is to provide its customers with annual comprehensive reports based on evaluation measures. More specifically, the agency intends to develop customized reports for certain county customers to demonstrate the program outcomes of youth placed in Woodland Hills. Evaluation results indicate to county consumers that Woodland Hills is a cost-effective placement with positive outcomes that should be considered when placing youth out of the home.

Questions and answers

Q: *What barriers have you experienced in using evaluation results, and how did you overcome those barriers?*

A: The barrier we encountered was that the evaluation focused on one specific customer (the county). This was our own agency decision, yet in retrospect, we should have conducted a comprehensive study reflecting all customers. To overcome this barrier, we chose to create our own report based on similar data that could be specific to one customer or to all combined. For other programs facing similar barriers, I would advise that when contracting the services of an outside evaluator, be sure the evaluation is comprehensive to the extent that the data is meaningful to all customers, not just one specifically. You will get more use out of the evaluation.

Q: *What advice do you have for programs hoping to use their evaluation results in similar ways?*

A: Evaluation is a worthwhile investment. While the costs are considerable up front, it is worth it in the end when you can be seen as a leader in your field for taking the challenge and realizing the importance of outcome evaluation. It is also a tremendous marketing asset when you have statistics to validate quality services.

Q: *What is the most important thing you have learned through your evaluation activities?*

A: Collecting the right data, having the technical infrastructure to support data integrity, and involving key staff in the development of the database and evaluation methods are important to a successful evaluation.

For Your Consideration:
Using Results to Market a Program

If you want to use program evaluation to market your program, you may want to consider the following:

- To whom do you want to market the evaluation findings?
- Will they consider the findings from your evaluation credible?
- Do you have good measures of costs and, if appropriate, economic benefits that justify spending money on the program versus another program?
- Can you show the "return on investment" for putting money into your program?
- Do you measure outcomes, not just satisfaction?
- Can you optimally "package" the evaluation findings—to get them to the audiences you want to reach, in the appropriate formats for those audiences?
- Are there ways to express the outcomes that will have greater impact on your audiences? For example, the Surgeon General drew attention to the impact of tobacco on the United States by describing it as the equivalent of a jumbo jet crash every day of the year.

Summary

In this chapter, we provided fourteen examples to describe and clarify the three primary uses of evaluation. While the most common use of evaluation findings is to improve programs and services, as these examples demonstrate, evaluation findings can also be used to influence policy and legislation and to market a program. These three primary uses are part of a larger mosaic of evaluation use uncovered in our conversations with forty organizations. We encourage you to consider other innovative ways of using evaluation in your own organization.

Promoting the Use of Evaluation Research Findings in Your Organization

"I like things to happen; and if they don't happen, I like to make them happen."

Winston Churchill[14]

THE STORIES IN THE PREVIOUS CHAPTER show very clearly the power of research findings to produce good things for your organization. You can motivate staff and volunteers. You can get other organizations and individuals engaged with your mission. You can increase referrals. You can increase revenues. You can demonstrate accountability and establish a sense of confidence in the work your organization does. You can involve the news media. And, of course, you can improve your effectiveness—which is the primary reason for systematically monitoring what you do and measuring your outcomes.

If that's the potential, then what, practically speaking, does it take to achieve this in your organization? How can you maximize the likelihood that you will do good program evaluation research and that you will use the results of that research to benefit your organization? Your organization should have at least three features:

1. *An evaluation culture.* You will have more success using evaluation if the process and use of evaluation has a positive, productive image within your organization's culture.

---

[14] Christopher Hassall, *Edward Marsh, Patron of the Arts: A Biography* (London, England: Longmans, Green, & Co. Ltd., 1959).

2. *Good information.* You can only really make use of program evaluation research when it is done well.

3. *A plan to use your results.* Make it a regular practice within your organization to identify ways to use program evaluation information.

Underlying these features is the notion that program evaluation, and its use, must become normal aspects of the daily life of your organization. Evaluation must be part of an ongoing process of designing your work, doing the work, learning what outcomes you have achieved, and then putting to use what you have learned.

Create an Evaluation Culture

You don't need a degree in psychology to know that individuals tend to do what they like and tend to avoid what they dislike. You also know that getting people to try something new requires motivation. They have to see the benefit, and they have to overcome the usual human fears and discomfort that change brings.

Therefore, a critical ingredient for developing and maintaining momentum within your organization to use program evaluation is the establishment of a positive, productive image of program evaluation and its use, within your organization's culture. Here are some ways to go about that.

Make sure all appropriate staff are involved in the development of the evaluation research that your organization does.

Involve staff from the beginning in the design of program evaluation. Involvement creates a sense of ownership. People feel better when they own a process than when they perceive that a process is imposed on them. In addition, involvement offers the opportunity for staff to become more comfortable with program evaluation and eliminate any fears they might have about how program evaluation will be used (or misused).

How to Create an Evaluation Culture

- Involve all appropriate staff in the development of evaluation
- Have staff regularly review, discuss, and act on evaluation findings
- Board members and top leadership must own and act on the evaluation findings

Have staff review and discuss program evaluation findings on a regular basis, and take action based on the results of this review and discussion.

Develop a process for regular review of program evaluation information and for discussions with staff concerning how to improve your organization's work. Very likely, your staff members want to improve what they do, and they want to increase the value of their work for the people your organization serves. Devote some staff meeting time to looking at the findings from your evaluation research. If client satisfaction ratings are lower than you like, ask staff to develop a strategy to do something different and improve the ratings. If you see that outcomes are better for one type of client than for another, ask staff why that might be. Then, take some action. It does not have to involve a major overhaul of your activities. Perhaps form a task force to explore different ways of providing service to the group with poorer outcomes, and then try providing service differently to see if that group can improve. This visible activity will set a tone and establish norms that nurture program evaluation and its use in your organization.

As one of our informants told us, "I guess the most important thing we learned is that we have to build a receptiveness and willingness to change based on evaluation results. We need to build in regular or annual self-reflection—so that the evaluation isn't just a snapshot, but continues to affect ourselves and the way we accomplish our mission. If it's only a onetime look, it's there and gone and it has limited effect. If it changes the organization to being consciously on the lookout for the kinds of things that the evaluation points out, it becomes incorporated into the organizational culture."

Top leadership should endorse the program evaluation process and use program evaluation findings.

Endorsement of program evaluation and its use by the board and senior management provides an official statement that evaluation is important. That's one step to take. Beyond that, the board and senior management need to model the behavior they want to see within the rest of the organization. They need to use the information creatively. This can occur, for example, in the following ways:

- Review and discuss the program evaluation findings at board meetings

- Require that reports about program activities include measures of outcomes

- Suggest ways that evaluation findings can go into public documents and communications to other agencies or the general public

- Meet with staff to discuss program evaluation findings and how to follow up with them

One informant offered this advice: "Be prepared to talk about the evaluation findings. The executive director should read the evaluation. It's amazing how many programs run evaluations and the top leadership has no clue of the results. Make sure that you understand and know what's in the evaluation because people are going to ask you. Be prepared to discuss your plan for improving."

Get Good Information

Invest in, and implement, research that is done well. The adage, "If it's worth doing, it's worth doing well," applies to program evaluation as well as many other things in life. In the stories in the previous chapter, you probably noticed that many of the informants with whom we spoke

How to Get Good Information

- Involve staff in evaluation design
- Allocate enough money to do the job well
- Hire competent evaluators
- Train staff for their roles in evaluation
- Clearly communicate results

emphasized the importance of *credibility*. You will only attain credibility if you do evaluation research that meets or exceeds standards that evaluation researchers and the public hold regarding the quality of the information, or evidence, that a study produces. Attaining credibility requires organizational commitment and organizational resources—both time and money. If you do an evaluation that is "quick and dirty," then staff within your organization won't find much reason to use it, and it won't carry much weight with people outside your organization.

So, you will need to spend the money necessary for good evaluation research, use competent talent (whether your own staff or an outside contractor) to do the evaluation research, and make whatever changes are necessary in your practices to ensure that you collect and report accurate information. Here are some ways to be sure you get good, useful information from your investment in evaluation.

Involve staff in the design of your organization's program evaluation research.

We already mentioned this with respect to promoting a positive image of evaluation and promoting a feeling of ownership among staff. We mention it again because the involvement of as many staff as possible in the design of an evaluation and in the interpretation of results greatly improves the quality of the evaluation. In the design stage, staff, who often take different viewpoints and have had different experiences, provide valuable feedback about the best ways to measure outcomes. In the interpretation stage, staff will provide alternative explanations for why the numbers came out as they did, so that the group can reach the best conclusions. Staff will also generate different ideas for improvement, so that the organization can try the most creative and promising approaches.

According to those we interviewed, involvement should include the building of a close relationship between at least some of the staff and whoever is doing the evaluation research. "Program staff and the research team need a very close and frequent relationship. This ensures that the two groups are in agreement on what's being evaluated and how it's being done," said one senior program officer. Another program coordinator told us: "It is essential that staff develop positive relationships with the members of their evaluation team. Through open and frequent communication with the researchers, staff can take an active role in the design of the evaluation and the interpretation of results. This helps to ensure that the final product is relevant, useful, and accurate in its depiction of the program's successes and challenges."

Some organizations, as you may have noted in the stories, also consider board involvement, along with staff involvement, very important. For example, one person we interviewed offered, "Both as a piece of advice and as the most important thing I learned, it's critical to build an evaluation plan into the initial operational plan and to get board members involved with the evaluation aspect of a project. Once the evaluation results come in, use them to develop the next stage of operational planning."

Staff development can also emerge as one of the additional benefits that accrue from doing program evaluation and having staff involved in it. As one of our informants explained, "Evaluation and research have served as a growth piece for our professional staff here as they have worked with our evaluator to learn more about the process. Staff would not have had the same opportunities for growth if we were not open to evaluation. We have a culture here that is committed to evaluation and research, making it a staff development piece as well."

Set aside sufficient money in the budget to carry out the evaluation design you have created.

It costs money to do evaluation research. Budget what's necessary, or do not expect to produce credible, useful results. When establishing a budget, get input from researchers experienced in evaluation so that you have a realistic projection of expenses.

If resources are limited, adjust your expectations for the evaluation to live within your means. Above all, make sure you do a credible job on whatever you decide to do. If you only have resources to look at a part of your program, or you can only measure some of your outcomes (but not all of them), then do so in a way that you obtain valid, reliable information within the limits of what you can afford. In this way, you will at least end up with something you can use, even though you would have preferred to be more comprehensive. Do not attempt to do a costly evaluation on insufficient funds, or you may end up with a lot of information that you and everyone else feel is of absolutely no value to use.

Hire a competent evaluation researcher.

Whether to do program evaluation on your own, or to hire someone else to do it for you—that's a decision you will have to make. No single answer applies to all organizations. However, all organizations do need to have someone with the necessary competence, whether a member of the regular staff or a person external to the organization. Make sure that you have the work done by someone whose training and experience match the needs of your organization.[15]

Train staff for their roles in the evaluation process.

Staff within the organization will have to collect information, store information, and perhaps enter information into computers. In addition, if you don't hire someone from the outside to analyze and report evaluation findings, your organization's staff will do that as well. It is important to train, and sometimes re-train, staff to carry out their duties in the collection, storing, analysis, and reporting of information.

---

[15] For guidance on choosing an evaluation researcher, see *The Manager's Guide to Program Evaluation: Planning, Contracting, and Managing for Useful Results* by Paul Mattessich (Saint Paul, MN: Fieldstone Alliance, 2003).

Clearly communicate results.

Communicating the results is as much a part of the evaluation process as design and data collection. Clear reporting enables staff and others to access the results of program evaluation for a variety of uses. It also provides a psychological reward for the effort required to do evaluation. To encourage use, be sure to communicate the information in common, everyday language rather than research or field-specific jargon.

Plan to Use Your Results

Establish a regular practice in your organization to identify specific ways to use program evaluation information. This will require some pioneering effort on your part. Most organizations do not do this on a regular basis. Many of the organizations we interviewed would admit that they stumbled upon new ways to use information. Now they emphasize the need to plan for how the evaluation findings will be used. This will require some additional time during the planning stages of an evaluation but, in the end, facilitates using the information from an evaluation to the full benefit for the organization.

Invite staff from different disciplines to review evaluation findings and, perhaps, to participate in the design or revision of your organization's evaluation.

In most organizations, meetings to review evaluation findings, as well as the initial meetings to design evaluation, typically include only program staff, top managers, and sometimes board members. Avoid this practice in your organization. You should include other members of your staff. For example:

- *Communications staff,* if you want to promote the use of findings for public relations, marketing, annual reports, messages to consumers and the public, and other communications uses.

- *Administrative support and scheduling staff*, if you want to generate ideas on how to use findings to improve the appearance, accessibility, and hospitality of your facilities for the people you serve.

- *Finance staff*, if you want to blend program evaluation findings with financial information for public relations, to make a stronger case for revenues you need, and to determine how to represent not just the benefit but also the cost-benefit of your organization's services.

- *Development staff and grant writers*, if you want to use evaluation findings to win grants and increase revenues in other ways.

Use a checklist to help your organization to think about new uses for program evaluation findings.

The checklist might include the types of uses we have reviewed in this book. Ask, How can we use this evaluation to

- Improve programs and services (the most important "use")?
- Influence policy or legislation?
- Increase revenue?
- Conduct public relations activities?
- Market the organizations?
- Influence funding decisions?
- Manage projects?
- Enable consumers to make better choices?
- Motivate staff?
- Shape other goals and decisions?

We offer this checklist to get you started thinking about ways to use evaluation in your organization. We agree with one project coordinator who said, "On the front end, have a very clear idea of what you want to use the results for and identify specific results that you are looking for or are anticipating before moving forward. Give yourself a reasonable timeline. Usually eight or nine detours occur, so if you expect that you'll be done in a certain amount of time, tack on 20 percent more time." To these comments we add, be open to discovering other ways to use the evaluation than you first planned. Many of the informants talked about figuring out innovative ways to use evaluation findings once they started thinking about use and participating in the evaluation process. The uses we described in this book are offered to expand our ideas on how evaluation findings can be used, but we have not described them all! We anticipate that once you begin thinking creatively about how evaluation findings can be used, you will discover many other uses than what we described in this volume.

Best Wishes for Productive Use of Program Evaluation!

"Action is eloquence, and the eyes of the ignorant
More learned than the ears."

Coriolanus, in Shakespeare's *Coriolanus*, Act III Sc 2

SHAKESPEARE REMINDS US that our actions "speak" more eloquently than words and have more impact. The findings from program evaluation research, if left in reports, are mere words on a page. When acted on, they demonstrate visibly to us and to others the impacts our programs can have. They empower others to take action as well—to influence policy, funding, consumer choice, and many other activities.

In the early chapters of this book, we reviewed features of program evaluation. We described how it can be integrated into the process of designing, monitoring, and improving programs. We indicated, from a strategic management perspective, what evaluation provides, what questions it answers, and what some of its strengths and limitations are.

Then, we discussed ways that organizations can use program evaluation findings. We moved beyond the typical, primary use—program improvement—and explored other strategic and operational uses of evaluation. In Chapter 4, short case examples illustrated in detail what organizations did, how they did it, what barriers they overcame, and so on. In Chapter 5, we suggested ways you can encourage the maximum use of evaluation within your organization.

We hope that these stories—real life examples of the successes and barriers your peers have faced with evaluation—have provided you with insight. We hope that the details of their stories offer some useful examples of how you can use program evaluation findings within your organization.

We wish you the best of luck and bid you on your way—with the wish that, in the words of Shakespeare, your action will be "eloquence." We hope your actions will inspire others to increase the impacts of their work through the creative uses of program evaluation that you have displayed!

Organizational Representatives for the Examples Listed in This Book

Nancy Latimer
Former Senior Program Officer
The McKnight Foundation

Mike McGrane
Director, Violence Prevention and Intervention Services (VPIS)
Amherst H. Wilder Foundation

Dr. Lawanda Ravoira
President and CEO
Practical Academic Cultural Education (PACE) Center for Girls, Florida office

Debbie Wilde
Executive Director
YouthZone

Shelley Lester
Program Development Coordinator
Shreveport-Bossier Community Renewal

Valentin Miafo-Donfack
Former Research and Analysis Associate
Shreveport-Bossier Community Renewal

Carol Arthur
Executive Director
Domestic Abuse Project

Kay Washington
Executive Director
Rural Opportunities, Inc., Pennsylvania Division

Sally Hopper
Executive Director
Dental Health for Arlington, Inc.

Angie Datta
Executive Director
StreetWise Partners, Inc.

Tanya Tull
President and CEO
Beyond Shelter, Inc.

Carol Seidenkranz
Coordinator, Family & Service Learning (Pike Lake Education Center)
Mounds View Even Start

Ellen Sachs Leicher
Founder
ESL Associates, LLC

Lesa Radtke
Executive Director
Woodland Hills

Kristi Lahti-Johnson
Administrative and Business Process Manager
Human Services and Public Health Department
(Former manager for Targeted Early Intervention)

Tony Rothschild
President and CEO
Common Ground Sanctuary

Index

f indicates figure

More results-oriented books from Fieldstone Alliance

The Manager's Guide to Program Evaluation

Here's how to get the information and insights you need to plan and conduct an evaluation that will help identify your organization's successes, share information with key audiences, and improve services. *The Manager's Guide to Program Evaluation* describes the types of information to collect, spells out the four phases of evaluation and the steps in each phase, and offers advice on hiring and working with a professional evaluator.

by Paul W. Mattessich   Item #069385   112 pages

A Funder's Guide to Evaluation

Forward-looking grantmakers and grantees are leveraging their evaluations, ensuring that the time and money spent ultimately improves effectiveness for everyone.

by Peter York   Item #069482   160 pages

Five Life Stages of Nonprofit Organizations

This useful guide helps you understand where your organization is in its life and how to avoid unnecessary struggles and act on opportunities to boost your organization's development.

by Judith Sharken Simon   Item #069229   128 pages

Benchmarking for Nonprofits

Benchmarking is the continuous process of measuring your organization against leaders to gain knowledge and insights that will help you improve. This book defines a formal, systematic, and reliable way to benchmark.

by Jason Saul   Item #069431   144 pages